商务英语口语实战丛书

国际商务英语口语

Spoken English for International Business

（修订本）

初级

主　编　廖国强　张礼贵　左　义
副主编　范　敏　龚蕴华　廖　旭

清华大学出版社
北京交通大学出版社
·北京·

内 容 简 介

本书共 9 个单元，主要内容包括商务接待、商务参观及产品介绍、远程商务接洽、商务约会、商务活动安排、商务咨询及说明、商务旅游、建立商务关系、涉外工作申请等涉外商务活动。

本书适用于高等院校商务英语及相关专业的学生，同时也适用于国际商务活动的从业者和爱好者。

本书封面贴有清华大学出版社防伪标签，无标签者不得销售。
版权所有，侵权必究。侵权举报电话：010-62782989 13501256678 13801310933

图书在版编目（CIP）数据

国际商务英语口语：初级 / 廖国强，张礼贵，左义主编. — 修订本. — 北京：北京交通大学出版社：清华大学出版社，2019.1（2023.9 修订）
ISBN 978-7-5121-1800-3

Ⅰ.① 国…　Ⅱ.① 廖…　② 张…　③ 左…　Ⅲ.① 国际商务-英语-口语　Ⅳ.① H319.9

中国版本图书馆 CIP 数据核字（2014）第 018719 号

国际商务英语口语（初级）
GUOJI SHANGWU YINGYU KOUYU（CHUJI）

责任编辑：	张利军
出版发行：	清华大学出版社　邮编：100084　电话：010-62776969　http://www.tup.com.cn
	北京交通大学出版社　邮编：100044　电话：010-51686414　http://www.bjtup.com.cn
印　刷　者：	北京鑫海金澳胶印有限公司
经　　　销：	全国新华书店
开　　　本：	185 mm×243 mm　　印张：9.5　　字数：284 千字
版 印 次：	2023 年 9 月第 1 版第 1 次修订　2023 年 9 月第 4 次印刷
定　　　价：	35.00 元

本书如有质量问题，请向北京交通大学出版社质监组反映。对您的意见和批评，我们表示欢迎和感谢。
投诉电话：010-51686043，51686008；传真：010-62225406；E-mail：press@bjtu.edu.cn。

前言 PREFACE

加入世界贸易组织,标志着我国对外开放新的全方位的推进。在经济全球化的新形势下,中国与世界各国的商务交流与合作也会更加频繁。作为一门通用的国际性语言,英语在国际商务交流中起着极其重要的作用。从事涉外商务工作的人员需要掌握好英语,特别是英语口语,才能更好地开展商务活动。

《国际商务英语口语》正是基于这样的背景而为从事对外经贸工作和其他涉外工作的人员及相关学习者编写的商务英语口语读本,既可以作为高等院校商务英语及相关专业学生的口语教材,又可以作为一种工具书,供相关的学习者参考模仿之用。

《国际商务英语口语》共3册,分为初级、中级和高级,主要内容涵盖了对外商务往来中最为常见的经典对话场景,基本上由易到难渐进地涉及了涉外贸易中所有主要的商务活动。

《国际商务英语口语》在选材上覆盖面广,代表性和针对性强,并且兼具实用性和生动性。在实用性方面,书中所选取的材料均为商务活动中最常见的场景,具有很强的实践性和可操作性,能够有效地帮助学习者进行针对性极强的训练并学以致用,符合应用型人才培养的要求。在生动性方面,书中所选取的材料具有较强的趣味性,易学易懂,能够充分地调动起不同层次学习者的学习兴趣。

《国际商务英语口语》在体系的编排上科学合理。

每单元的开始部分均提供了与本单元话题相关的文化背景，以帮助学习者对此话题有一个更加准确的把握。每单元的主体是日常商务对话的经典范例及常用词汇、句型，学习者可以此为模板学习并熟练掌握其中的一些对话技巧。每单元还就对话中出现的语言难点及重要的国际商务知识给出了详尽的注释，以帮助学习者更深入地理解本单元的主题。每单元的课后练习也紧紧围绕本单元的话题展开，主要有"根据中文提示补全对话"和"根据提供的对话背景模仿特定人物进行情景对话"两大类实操性训练。

为了让学习者能够在涉外商务活动中有效地进行交流，每单元后还附有本单元对话的译文，以供学习者参阅。为了让学习者能够更好地掌握相关话题的对话技巧，每单元最后均提供了与之相关的扩展阅读材料，并留有让学习者参与讨论的问题。

本书为《国际商务英语口语》的初级本，共9个单元，主要内容涵盖商务接待、商务参观及产品介绍、远程商务接洽、商务约会、商务活动安排、商务咨询及说明、商务旅游、建立商务关系、涉外工作申请等涉外商务活动。

本书以二维码的形式动态地向读者提供相关的教学资源，读者可先扫描封底上的防盗码获得资源读取权限，然后再根据自身的学习需求，通过扫描每单元开始处的二维码，获取并使用相关的教学资源。例如，本书中所有的对话均配有地道的MP3录音，学习者扫描二维码后即可收听，并可对照本书的教学材料进行对话模仿训练。

本书在编写过程中参考了大量的文献资料，在此向这些文献资料的作者表示衷心的感谢。编者也殷切地希望本书能够对相关读者的商务英语学习有所帮助。然而，鉴于编者水平有限，书中难免有错漏之处，恳请广大读者批评指正。

编者

2023年9月

目录 CONTENTS

Unit 1   Business Reception
商务接待 ·· 1

Unit 2   Business Visit and Products Introduction
商务参观及产品介绍 ······························ 15

Unit 3   Distant Business Communication
远程商务接洽 ·· 25

Unit 4   Business Appointment
商务约会 ·· 37

Unit 5   Business Agenda
商务活动安排 ·· 49

Unit 6   Business Inquiry and Explanation
商务咨询及说明 ······································ 63

Unit 7   Business Travelling
商务旅游 ·· 77

Unit 8   Building up Business Relations
建立商务关系 ·· 95

Unit 9   Application for Foreign Jobs
涉外工作申请 ·· 115

Appendix A   **Glossary**
词汇表 ·· 132

References
参考文献 ·· 143

Unit

1

Business Reception
商务接待

Learning Resources

Warming-up

A receptionist is the first person that hotel guests see or talk to when they arrive or ring to make a booking. A hotel receptionist therefore has an important job of making people feel welcome, being efficient and dealing professionally with enquiries. In this job, the tasks are likely to include welcoming guests as they arrive, allocating them a room and handing out keys to guests or porters, taking and passing on messages. He will probably also have to put together the guest's bill, take payment and help guests with any special requests. A receptionist sometimes orders taxis for guests and books excursions on request, such as theatre or sightseeing trips.

A receptionist needs to be welcoming, friendly and helpful, efficient and professional, well-organized and able to handle several tasks at once.

The work of a receptionist is interesting and varied. The work is also important because the receptionist is the first person visitors see when they come to a firm. So the receptionist gives them the first impression of the firm.

Dialogues

Dialogue 1   Receiving Guests at the Airport

The Fortune Hotel airport representative (AR) receives a guest (G) at the airport.

G: Excuse me, are you the Fortune Hotel airport representative?
AR: Yes, Mr. ...?
G: I'm Robert Hilton from America.
AR: My name is Su Hui. I'm here to meet you. Welcome to Shanghai!
G: Glad to meet you.
AR: The pleasure is mine. Is this your first visit to China, Mr. Hilton?
G: Yes. It's my first visit. I'm looking forward to seeing your beautiful country.
AR: I hope you will have a pleasant stay here.
G: Thank you. I'm sure I will.

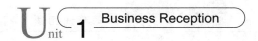

AR: Is this all your baggage?
G: Yes, it's all here.
AR: We have a car over there to take you to our hotel.
G: That's fine.
AR: Let me help you with that suitcase. Shall we go?
G: Yes, thank you for all your trouble.
AR: No trouble at all. This way, please.

Dialogue 2 Receiving Guests at the Reception Desk of the Company

Rose (R) is the receptionist of Modern Office Ltd. Mr. Li (L) hasn't an appointment, but he'd like to see Mr. Shelli. Maria (M) is Mr. Shelli's secretary.

L: Good morning.
R: Good morning. Oh, Mr. Li. How are you?
L: I'm fine, thanks, and you?
R: Oh, busy as usual. Do you want to see Mr. Shelli?
L: Yes, please.
R: Do you have an appointment?
L: Er... No, I haven't. You see, I only arrived in the country this morning.
R: Well, I know he's busy at the moment, but I'll ask his secretary when he'll be free. Please sit down.
L: Thank you.
   (Dials)
M: Mr. Shelli's office.
R: Oh, hello, Maria. It's the reception. I have Mr. Li here. He hasn't an appointment, but he'd like to see Mr. Shelli. When will he be free?
M: Let me see... Well, hmmm, he'll be free about 12:30. Can Mr. Li wait for a while?
R: *(To Mr. Li)* Mr. Shelli will be free about half past twelve. Can you wait for a while?
L: What's the time now?
R: It's nearly 12:00.
L: Oh, that's fine. I'll wait.
R: *(To Maria)* Maria, Mr. Li will wait.

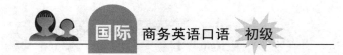

M: Right. I'll fetch him when Mr. Shelli's free.
R: Thanks. *(Replaces the phone) (To Mr. Li)* She'll come and fetch you later.
L: Thank you.

Dialogue 3   Receiving Guests at the Hotel

The receptionist (R) of the hotel welcomes the guest (G).

R: Good afternoon, sir. Welcome to our hotel. May I help you?
G: Yes. I booked a room one week ago.
R: May I have your name please, sir?
G: John Smith.
R: Just a moment, sir. Yes, we do have a reservation for you, Mr. Smith. A city view single room with bath. You've paid 2,000 yuan as a deposit. Is that correct?
G: That's it.
R: Would you please fill in this registration card, sir?
G: Sure. Here you are. I think I've filled in everything correctly.
R: Let me see… name, address, nationality, forwarding address, passport number, signature and date of departure. Oh, here, sir. You forget to fill in the date of departure. May I fill it in for you? You are leaving on…
G: October 24.
R: May I see your passport, please? Thank you, sir. Now everything is in order. And here is your key, Mr. Smith. Your room number is 1107. It's on the 11th floor and your room rate is RMB 500 per night. Here is your key card with all the information on your booking, the hotel services and the hotel rules and regulations on it. Please make sure that you have it with you all the time. You need to show it when you sign for your meals and drinks in the restaurants and the bars.
G: Yes, I'll keep it with care. Thank you.
R: I hope you enjoy your stay with us.

Dialogue 4   Receiving Guests at the Fair

Mr. Brown (B) and Ms. Anderson (A) are talking at the Fair.

Unit 1 Business Reception

B: Good afternoon. I am Robert Brown, the Import Manager of Atlantic Industries Ltd., Sidney, Australia. This is my card.

A: Good afternoon, Mr. Brown. I am Meese Anderson, manager of the sales department.

B: Nice to see you, Ms. Anderson.

A: Nice to see you too, Mr. Brown. Won't you sit down?

B: Thank you.

A: What would you like, tea or coffee?

B: I'd prefer coffee if you don't mind.

A: Is it your first trip to the Fair, Mr. Brown?

B: No, it's the fourth time.

A: Good. Is there anything you find changed about the Fair?

B: Yes, a great deal. The business scope has been broadened, and there are more visitors than ever before.

A: Really, Mr. Brown? Did you find anything interesting?

B: Oh, yes. Quite a bit. But we are especially interested in your products.

A: We are glad to hear that. What items are you particularly interested in?

B: Women's dresses. They are fashionable and suit Australian women well, too. If they are of high quality and the prices are reasonable, we'll purchase large quantities of them. Will you please quote us a price?

A: All right.

Words and Expressions

baggage   *n.*   行李
suitcase   *n.*   手提箱，衣箱
appointment   *n.*   约定，约会
free   *a.*   有空的
fetch   *v.*   接来，取来
book   *v.*   预订
reservation   *n.*   预订

deposit   *n.*   储蓄，保证金，订金
registration   *n.*   登记
forwarding address   转投地址，转寄地址
sign   *v.*   签单
business scope   经营范围
quote   *v.*   开（价）

1. 许多规模较大的公司都会有一个接待员,我们通常称作前台(receptionist)。可不要小瞧这个职位,前台的工作也是复杂多样的。而且有个好的前台对公司来说非常重要,因为前台是访客在公司接触到的第一个人,前台可能会影响客人对公司的第一印象。
2. 英美人是很尊重别人的个人隐私(privacy)的。他们一般不打听对方的私事,包括婚姻及家庭情况(问候家人例外),更忌讳问别人的年龄和收入。特别是对女性,更不能无缘无故地随意问及年龄。在接待英美客人时,要特别注意不同的文化风俗习惯。
3. I hope you will have a pleasant stay here.
   希望您在我们这里过得愉快。(客人入住宾馆前)
   I hope you are enjoying your stay with us.
   希望您在我们宾馆过得愉快。(客人在宾馆逗留期间)
   I hope you have enjoyed your stay with us.
   希望您在我们宾馆过得愉快。(客人离开宾馆时)

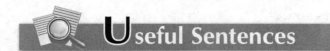

1. I'd like to book a double room for Tuesday next week.
   下周二我想订一个双人房间。
2. What's the price difference?
   两种房间的价格有什么不同?
3. A double room with a front view is 140 dollars per night, and one with a rear view is 115 dollars per night.
   一间双人房朝阳面的每晚 140 美元,背阴面的每晚 115 美元。
4. I think I'll take the one with a front view then.
   我想我还是要阳面的吧。
5. How long will you be staying?
   您打算住多久?
6. We'll be leaving Sunday morning.
   我们将在星期天上午离开。
7. And we look forward to seeing you next Tuesday.

Unit 1 Business Reception

我们盼望下周二见到您。

8. I'd like to book a single room with bath from the afternoon of October 4 to the morning of October 10.
   我想订一个带浴室的单人房间，10月4日下午到10月10日上午用。

9. We do have a single room available for those dates.
   我们确实有一个单间，在这段时间可以用。

10. What is the rate, please?
    请问房费多少？

11. The current rate is $50 per night.
    现行房费是50美元一天。

12. What services come with that?
    这个价格包括哪些服务项目呢？

13. That sounds not bad at all. I'll take it.
    听起来还不错。这个房间我要了。

14. By the way, I'd like a quiet room away from the street if it is possible.
    顺便说一下，如有可能我想要一个不临街的安静房间。

15. Welcome to our hotel.
    欢迎光临。

16. So you have got altogether four pieces of baggage?
    您一共带了4件行李，是不是？

17. Let me have a check again.
    让我再看一下。

18. The Reception Desk is straight ahead.
    接待处就在前面。

19. After you, please.
    您先请。

20. Excuse me, where can I buy some cigarettes?
    劳驾，我到哪儿可以买到香烟？

21. There is a shop on the ground floor.
    一楼有个商店。

22. It sells both Chinese and foreign cigarettes.
    在那儿可以买到中国香烟和外国香烟。

23. Can I also get some souvenirs there?
    也可以买到纪念品吗？

24. There is a counter selling all kinds of souvenirs.

有个柜台出售各种各样的纪念品。

25. Excuse me, where is the restaurant?
    劳驾，请问餐厅在哪儿？
26. We have a Chinese restaurant and a western-style restaurant. Which one do you prefer?
    我们有中餐厅和西餐厅，您愿意去哪个？
27. I'd like to try some Chinese food today.
    今天我想尝尝中国菜。
28. Good. Could you please fill in this booking form? We need your full address and a deposit of 20 percent. You can pay by cash or credit card or cheque.
    好的。请您填一下这张预订单，好吗？请填写您的详细地址并交付20%的订金。您可以用现金、信用卡或是支票支付。
29. I've come to make sure that your stay in Beijing is a pleasant one.
    我特地为你们安排以确保你们在北京的逗留愉快。
30. You're going out of your way for us, I believe.
    我相信这是对我们的特殊照顾了。
31. It's just the matter of the schedule, that is, if it is convenient for you right now.
    如果你们觉得方便的话，我想现在讨论一下日程安排的问题。
32. I think we can draw up a tentative plan now.
    我认为现在可以先草拟一套临时方案。
33. If he wants to make any changes, minor alternations can be made then.
    如果他有什么意见的话，我们还可以对计划稍加修改。
34. Is there any way of ensuring we'll have enough time for our talks?
    如何保证我们能有充足的时间来谈判呢？
35. So our evenings will be quite full then?
    那么我们在晚上也安排满了活动吗？
36. We'll leave some evenings free, that is, if it is all right with you.
    如果你们愿意的话，我们想留几个晚上供你们自由支配。
37. We'd have to compare notes on what we've discussed during the day.
    我们需要研究讨论一下白天谈判的情况。
38. That'll put us both in the picture.
    这样双方都能了解全面的情况。
39. Then we'd have some ideas of what you'll be needing.
    那么我们就会心中有点儿数，知道你们需要什么了。
40. I can't say for certain off-hand.
    我还不能马上说定。

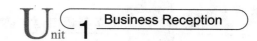

41. Better have something we can get our hands on rather than just spend all our time talking.
    有些实际材料拿到手总比坐着闲聊强。

42. It'll be easier for us to get down to facts then.
    这样就容易进行实质性的谈判了。

43. But wouldn't you like to spend an extra day or two here?
    但是,你们不愿意在这儿多待一两天吗?

44. I'm afraid that won't be possible, much as we'd like to.
    尽管我们很想这样做,但恐怕不行了。

45. We've got to report back to the head office.
    我们还要回去向总部汇报情况呢。

46. Thank you for your cooperation.
    感谢你们的合作。

47. We've arranged our schedule without any trouble.
    我们已经很顺利地把活动日程安排好了。

48. Here is a copy of itinerary we have worked out for you and your friends. Would you please have a look at it?
    这是我们为您和您的朋友拟定的活动日程安排。请过目一下,好吗?

49. If you have any questions on the details, feel free to ask.
    如果对某些细节有意见的话,请提出来。

50. I can see you have put a lot of time into it.
    我相信你在制定这个计划上一定花了不少精力吧。

51. We really wish you'll have a pleasant stay here.
    我们真诚地希望你们在这里过得愉快。

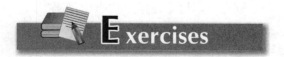

I. Complete the following dialogues.

1. **A:** Good to see you too, Tom. How was your flight?
   B: _____!
   (很好。在机场没有延误,这一路也很舒适。我还在飞机上睡了一会儿呢!)

2. **A:** Good. Do you have any jet lag?

B: _____
_____.
（现在不会了。我在韩国、日本的时候，就渐渐适应时差了，所以应该没有时差问题。）

II Situational practice.

The situation: You, the representative of your company, are expected to welcome David Brown, who comes from America, at the airport, and then accompany him from the airport to the hotel. After that, you accompany him to your company where you will introduce him to your general manager, Li Wei.

The task: Design possible dialogues according to the situation mentioned above.

对话汉译

▶ 对话 1 机场接待

福庆酒店的机场代表（AR）在机场迎接客人（G）。

G: 请问，您是福庆酒店的机场代表吗？
AR: 是的，您是……
G: 我是来自美国的罗伯特·希尔顿。
AR: 我叫苏辉，专程来这儿接您的。欢迎您到上海来。
G: 很高兴见到您。
AR: 很高兴见到您。希尔顿先生，这是您第一次来中国吗？
G: 是的，第一次。我一直想亲眼看看这个美丽的国家。
AR: 希望您在这儿过得愉快。
G: 谢谢，我想会的。
AR: 这是您所有的行李吗？
G: 是的，都在这儿。
AR: 我们的车在那儿，用来接您到酒店的。
G: 好的。
AR: 我帮您提箱子。可以走了吗？
G: 好的，谢谢，辛苦您了。

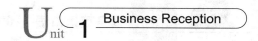

AR: 没什么。这边请。

▶ 对话 2　公司前台接待

罗斯（R）是现代办公公司的前台。李先生（L）没有预约但想拜访谢力先生。玛利亚（M）是谢力先生的秘书。

L: 早上好！
R: 早上好！李先生，近来可好？
L: 很好，谢谢。您呢？
R: 还是忙呗。您想见谢礼力先生吗？
L: 是的，请转告。
R: 您预约了吗？
L: 没有。您知道我今天早上刚到这个国家。
R: 我知道他现在很忙。不过，我先问一下他秘书，看他是否有空。您请坐。
L: 谢谢！
　　（拨号）
M: 您好，这是谢力先生办公室。
R: 玛利亚，我是前台。我们这儿有一位李先生想见谢力先生，但没有预约，不知谢力先生何时有空？
M: 我查一下，哦，谢力先生十二点半有空。李先生能等一会儿吗？
R: （对李先生说）谢力先生十二点半有空，您能等一会儿吗？
L: 现在什么时间？
R: 快到十二点了。
L: 那好，我就等会儿。
R: （对玛利亚说）玛利亚，李先生说可以等。
M: 好的，谢力先生忙完了我就来接他。
R: 谢谢。（挂上电话）（对李先生说）玛利亚等会儿来接您。
L: 谢谢！

▶ 对话 3　酒店接待

酒店前台（R）欢迎客人（G）。

R: 先生，下午好！欢迎您入住我们的酒店。请问我能为您做什么？

11

G: 好的,一周前我预订了一个房间。
R: 请问您的尊姓大名?
G: 约翰·史密斯。
R: 先生,请稍等。是的,史密斯先生,我们有您的预订。您订的是一个带浴室的城市观景单间并已支付2 000元人民币的订金,对吗?
G: 是的。
R: 先生,请填一下登记卡,好吗?
G: 好的,我觉得每一项都填好了,给你。
R: 我看一下……姓名、住址、国籍、转寄地址、护照编号、签名、离店时间。哦,先生,离店时间还没填呢,我可以帮您填吗?您离店的时间是……
G: 10月24日。
R: 我可以看一下您的护照吗?谢谢。一切都办好了。这是您的房间钥匙。史密斯先生,您的房间号是1107,在11楼,房费每晚500元人民币。这是您的钥匙卡,上面有房间预订信息、酒店服务指南以及酒店的有关规章制度,请务必时刻随身携带,您在餐厅和酒吧签单时需出示此卡。
G: 好的,我一定小心保管。谢谢!
R: 祝您在这里过得愉快!

对话4 展会接待

布朗先生(B)与安德森女士(A)在展会上谈话。

B: 下午好!我是罗伯特·布朗,是澳大利亚悉尼大西洋工业有限公司进口部经理。这是我的名片。
A: 布朗先生,下午好!我是米斯·安德森,销售部的经理。
B: 见到您很高兴,安德森女士。
A: 布朗先生,我也很高兴见到您。请坐。
B: 谢谢。
A: 您喝茶还是咖啡?
B: 如不介意,请来杯咖啡吧。
A: 布朗先生,这是您第一次参加展会吗?
B: 不,这是第四次了。
A: 太好了。您发现展会有什么变化吗?
B: 有啊,变化很大。经营范围扩大了,而且参观者也比以往多了很多。
A: 布朗先生,真的吗?您有没有发现感兴趣的商品?

Unit 1 Business Reception

B: 哦，是的，有很多。我们对你们的产品尤其感兴趣。
A: 听您这样说我们非常高兴。您对什么产品尤其感兴趣呢？
B: 女士连衣裙。这些连衣裙的款式不仅时髦，而且很适合澳洲妇女穿着。如果这些衣服质量好，价格合理，我们将大量订购。您能开个价吗？
A: 好的。

Extended Reading

1. 相互介绍认识的基本原则

(1) A man is always introduced to a woman.
    男士通常会先被介绍给女士。
(2) A young person is always introduced to an older person.
    年轻人通常会先被介绍给年龄大的人。
(3) A less important person is always introduced to a more important person.
    地位不太高的人通常会先被介绍给地位高一些的人。

2. 谁先坐下

When a client is coming for business purpose, the host should stand up and receive the guest, and offer a chair and a cup of coffee. He shouldn't sit down until the guest takes a seat. When the guest rises to leave, the host should go with him as far as the door of the office or the elevator. The executive doesn't rise for his secretary or coworkers in the office.

如果客户是为商务目的而来，主人要起身接待客人，给他让一个座位并且倒上一杯咖啡。而且，在客人落座之前主人不能坐下。当客人起身告辞时，主人需将客人送到办公室门口或者电梯口。而总经理则不需为秘书或者办公室同事站起来。

3. 正确地握手

A handshake can create a feeling of immediate friendliness of instant irritation between two strangers. The proper handshake is brief, but there should be firmness and warmth in the clasp. It should always be accompanied by a direct look into the eyes of the person whom you shake your hands with.

握手可以使本来陌生的两个人马上建立起友谊。正确的握手要迅捷，但是在握手的瞬间应有力度并且充满热情。在握手的同时要直视对方。

4. 如何交谈

While speaking with a visitor during an appointment, you should bear in mind that listening is as essential as talking. Nothing is more irritating and insulting to a visitor to have an appointment interrupted by continual phone calls.

在与你约见的来访者交谈时，要记住倾听与交谈一样重要。没有比不停地被电话打断更加令来访者恼怒和感到羞辱的事了。

You need instruct your assistant to hold all calls except emergencies until the end of your appointment. If your phone system includes a "message taking" feature, be sure to make use of it. If the caller is veering too far away from the subject, you might say: "Since I have another appointment in a few minutes, I'd like to discuss our primary concern."

在交谈结束之前，你要告诉你的助理帮你接听所有的电话，除非有特别紧急的事情。如果你的电话系统带有"留言"功能，记得使用它。如果来电者讲话离题太远，你可以说："因为我几分钟后还有一个约会，我们还是讨论我们重点关注的问题吧。"

Topic discussion:

What are the most important factors about culture and manners when one receives guests from English-speaking countries and regions?

常用词汇和短语

departure	n. 离开	negotiation	n. 谈判，磋商
extension	n. 延长（日期），（电话）分机	passport	n. 护照
		place of issue	n. 颁发地点
forward	v. 发送，寄发	regulation	n. 规章，规定，条例
nationality	n. 国籍	signature	n. 签名

Unit 2

Business Visit and Products Introduction

商务参观及产品介绍

Learning Resources

Warming-up

Visiting the factory of a company is important and necessary because it is a direct way of getting wanted information, such as equipment, quality of the workers, management and so on, which determines the final quality of the products or services. Consequently, it helps to achieve success in the coming trade.

Dialogues

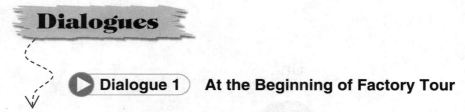

Dialogue 1　At the Beginning of Factory Tour

A and B are talking during the factory tour.

A: We'd like to welcome everyone to the Michelson Tools factory site, and thank everyone for being here today. My name is Paul Shafer. I'll be showing you around today. Please feel free to ask questions at any point during our tour. I'll be happy to answer questions for you.

B: Is it really necessary to wear all this protective gear?

A: That's an excellent question. I'll bet your wondering why we ask you to wear hard hats and safety goggles while you're in the plant. The reason is simple — we care about your safety and we want to ensure there are no injuries today. As you will see, to maintain a high level of safety, we also require all of our staff to wear similar protective gear.

B: How long will the tour take?

A: It should take about twenty minutes to go through the main plant, and maybe another ten to take a look at the laboratory. All together our tour should last about half an hour.

B: OK.

A: Well, if you don't have any questions, shall we get started? If you'll follow me, first I'll take you to the site of our semi-conductor system...

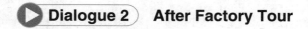

Dialogue 2　After Factory Tour

B shows the factory to his customer A.

Unit 2 Business Visit and Products Introduction

A: It was very kind of you to give me a tour of the place. It gave me a good idea of your product range.

B: It's a pleasure to show our factory to our customers. What's your general impression, may I ask?

A: Very impressive, indeed, especially the speed of your NW Model.

B: That's our latest development — a product with high performance. We put it on the market just two months ago.

A: The machine gives you an edge over your competitors, I guess.

B: Certainly. No one can match us as far as speed is concerned.

A: Could you give me some brochures for that machine? And the price if possible.

B: Right. Here is our sales catalog and literature.

A: Thank you. I think we may be able to work together in the future.

Dialogue 3   Business Visit

A is talking to B about factory tour.

A: Would you like to look around our factory some time?
B: That's a good idea.
A: I can set up a tour next week.
B: Just let me know which day.
   …
A: Thanks for coming today.
B: I've been looking forward to this.
A: You'll have to wear this hard hat for the tour.
B: This one seems a little small for me.
A: Here, try this one.
B: That's better.
A: We can start at any time you're ready.
B: I'm all set.
A: The tour will take about an hour and a half. We can start over here.
B: I'll just follow you.
A: Please stop me if you have any questions.
B: I will.
A: Watch your head as you go through the door there.

B: Thank you.

…

A: That's the end of the tour.

B: It was very informative.

A: Just let me know if you want to bring anyone else.

B: I'd like to have my boss go through the plant some day.

Dialogue 4   About Products

A accompanies B during the factory tour.

A: Put on the helmet, please.

B: Do we need to put on the jackets too?

A: You'd better, to protect your clothes. Now please watch your step.

B: Thank you. Is the production line fully automated?

A: Well, not fully automated.

B: I see. How do you control the quality?

A: All products have to go through five checks in the whole manufacturing process.

B: What's the monthly output?

A: One thousand units per month now. But we'll be making 1,200 units beginning with October.

B: What's your usual percentage of rejects?

A: About 2% in normal operations.

B: That's wonderful. Is that where the finished products come off?

A: Yes. Shall we take a break now?

Words and Expressions

protective gear 防护装备	helmet *n.* 安全帽，头盔
safety goggle 护目镜	production line 生产线
semi-conductor system 半导体生产系统	output *n.* 产量
	percentage of rejects 不合格率
brochure *n.* 小册子	

Unit 2 Business Visit and Products Introduction

1. 了解对方客户的商品生产主体——工厂——是对外贸易中必不可少的一环。工厂的设备、规模和工人的素质以及决策者的管理能力都决定着以后产品的质量和信誉。作为索取资料、电话传真问询、浏览网页的必要补充步骤，参观工厂可以让客户最直接、最客观地了解生产方公司，对日后的贸易成功意义重大。
2. 商务参观时要注意：① 针对性，参观对自己是最重要、最有实际价值的项目；② 量力而行，同时兼顾费用的高低、时间的长短、路途的远近及当时工作繁忙的具体程度；③ 照顾个人意愿；④ 讲究客随主便，参观项目应由宾主双方共同商定。

1. We look forward to our tour of your plant.
   我们盼望着参观你们的工厂。
2. If there is not too much trouble, we would like to talk to some of the technicians.
   如果不是太麻烦的话，我们想与一些技术员谈一谈。
3. We learned a lot about your facilities and the process of wine making.
   关于你们的酿酒设备和酿酒流程，我们了解了不少情况。
4. We're interested in learning about your food-making and packaging process.
   我们想向你们学习食品加工和包装流程。
5. It was very kind of you to give me a tour of the plant.
   谢谢你陪同我参观工厂。
6. You will surely know the products better after the visit.
   参观工厂后你对我们的产品肯定会更了解。
7. Let me give you this list of departments first.
   我先给你这份各个部门的清单。
8. Next to each department is its location and the name of the manager.
   在每个部门的旁边都标有其具体位置和经理的姓名。
9. Please let us know when you will be free so that we can arrange the tour for you.
   请告诉我们你们什么时候有空，我们好作参观安排。
10. Does the plant work with everything from the raw material to the finished product?

从原料到成品都是工厂自己生产吗？

11. I will give you a complete picture of our operation.
    我将使你完全了解我们厂的运作情况。

12. It's always a real pleasure to show our plant to our friends in the same industry and exchange ideas with them.
    能够把我们的工厂展示给同行的朋友并且与他们交换意见，总是一件非常愉快的事。

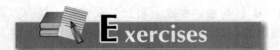

I Complete the following dialogues.

1. A: _____.
   （材料很好、设计时尚、做工优秀。）
   B: I see. The quality seems all right, but your prices are too high.

2. A: _____?
   （我们一定要戴上头盔和面具吗？）
   B: I'm afraid you must.

II Situational practice.

The situation: Mr. William Taylor, president of one corporation, and Mr. James Rogers, marketing manager, would like to visit Beijing to continue the discussions on a joint venture. They plan to stay in China about a week and visit your factory.

The task: Create a dialogue about the tour.

对话汉译

对话 1 参观开始

A 和 B 在参观工厂过程中交谈。

A: 欢迎大家来到迈克尔逊工厂，非常感谢今天到场的诸位嘉宾。我叫保罗·夏飞，今

Unit 2 Business Visit and Products Introduction

天由我来带领大家参观。参观期间请随时提问,我乐于为大家解答。
B: 真的有必要戴上这种防护装备吗?
A: 这个问题提得不错,我敢说你们一定想知道参观工厂时我们为什么要求你们戴上安全帽和护目镜,原因很简单,我们担心诸位的安全,要确保今天不出现任何受伤现象。你们还会看到,为了保证绝对安全,我们要求所有员工也戴上同样的防护装备。
B: 多长时间能参观完?
A: 参观主要生产车间需要 20 分钟,也许再有 10 分钟去看一下实验室,总共大约需要半个小时。
B: 好的。
A: 好了,如果没有问题,我们可以开始吗?请大家跟着我走,我们先去参观半导体生产车间……

▶ 对话 2 参观后

B 带领客户 A 参观工厂。

A: 谢谢你们陪同我看了整个工厂。这次参观使我对你们的产品范围有了一个很好的了解。
B: 带我们的客户来参观工厂是我们的荣幸。不知道您总体印象如何?
A: 很好,尤其是你们的 NW 型机器的速度。
B: 那是我们新开发的产品,性能很好。两个月前刚投放市场。
A: 和你们的竞争对手相比,我想这机器可以让你们多占一个优势。
B: 当然。就速度而言,目前没有厂家能和我们相比。
A: 能给我一些那种机器配套的小册子吗?如有可能,还有价格。
B: 好的。这是我们的销售目录和说明书。
A: 谢谢。我想也许将来我们可以合作。

▶ 对话 3 商务参观

A 和 B 谈论参观工厂的有关情况。

A: 什么时候来看看我们的工厂吧?
B: 好啊。
A: 我可以安排在下个星期参观。
B: 决定好哪一天就告诉我。
 …………

A: 谢谢您今天的光临。
B: 好久以前就想来看看你们的工厂了。
A: 参观时必需戴上这安全帽。
B: 这顶我戴好像小了一点。
A: 喏，试试这一顶。
B: 好多了。
A: 只要您准备好了，我们随时可以开始。
B: 我都准备好了。
A: 这次参观大概需要一个半小时。我们可以从这里开始。
B: 我跟着你就是。
A: 有任何问题，请随时叫我停下来。
B: 好的。
A: 经过那儿的门时，小心别撞到头。
B: 谢谢。

....

A: 参观就此结束了。
B: 真是获益良多。
A: 如果您要带别人来，请随时通知我。
B: 我打算叫我老板哪天也过来看看。

对话 4　关于产品

A 陪同 B 参观工厂。

A: 请戴上安全帽。
B: 我们还得穿上夹克吗？
A: 最好穿上，以免弄脏你的衣服。请留神脚下。
B: 谢谢。生产线都是全自动的吗？
A: 哦，不是全部自动的。
B: 哦，那你们如何控制质量呢？
A: 所有产品在整个生产过程中都必须通过五道质量检查关。
B: 月产量多少？
A: 目前每月 1 000 套，但从十月份开始每月将生产 1 200 套。
B: 每月不合格率通常是多少？
A: 正常情况下为 2% 左右。
B: 那太了不起了。成品从那边出来吗？

Unit 2　Business Visit and Products Introduction

A: 是的，现在我们需要稍微休息一下吗？

Extended Reading

Questions for Visiting Factory

(1) When did the factory build up?
(2) What about the factory's monthly capacity? What about the factory's monthly capacity offered to our customers?
(3) What's the main product in factory?
(4) Who are the managers and how about their background?
(5) What's the factory's main customers? How about its market?
(6) Did the factory pass other customer's evaluation?
(7) What about the lead time?
(8) What is the scale and how many workers?
(9) Is the factory a vertical maker or contract factory?
(10) Who's the key person handling orders?

Topic discussion:

What do you consider when you are visiting a factory?

 常用词汇和短语

accessory	n. 零件，配件	boost	v. 提高
administrative	a. 行政的，管理的	brand	n. 牌子，商标
anniversary	n. 周年纪念	capacity	n. 生产量，生产力
annual	a. 每年的，年度的	concerned	a. 有关的
assembly line	装配线	counter sample	对等样品
automated	a. 机械化的，自动的	edge	n. 优势，优越之处
bad quality	劣质	facility	n. 设备

23

first-class quality 头等质量，头等品质	performance *n.* （机器等）工作性能
gross *a.* 总的，毛的，总共的	raw material 原料
high quality 高质量	sales by sample 凭样品买卖
impressive *a.* 给人印象深刻的	sample for reference 参考样品
inspection *n.* 检验	sampling *n.* 抽样，取样
lag *v.* 走得慢，落后	section *n.* 部门，处，科，组
literature *n.* 商品说明书之类的印刷宣传品	shift *n.* 轮班
	square meter 平方米
merge *v.* （企业、团体等）合并	tip-top quality 第一流的质量
monthly *a.* 每月的	trademark *n.* 商标
output *n.* 产量，出产	warehouse *n.* 仓库

Unit

3

Distant Business Communication

远程商务接洽

Learning Resources

Warming-up

You have the ability to call anyone, anytime, anywhere if you know how to do it correctly. Attract new clients and grow your business by using these tips for better calling.

1. **Do your homework.** When making a call you have to be as prepared as possible.

2. **Set small and obtainable goals.** If you are reluctant or apprehensive about making phone calls to an unfamiliar person, set small goals at first until you get the hang of things.

3. **It's not about you, it's about them.** It is crucial to know in advance how your product or service is going to help your customers.

4. **Be persistent and enthusiastic.** A smile actually causes a physiological change in the tone of your voice because smiling elongates the vocal chords. Your energy and enthusiasm is easily recognizable over the phone, so it's OK to be excited about your business.

5. **Be memorable and follow-up.** In order to reach a decision maker or your target audience you need to stand out of the crowd.

Finally, remember to have fun and take risks. When you believe in yourself and your company, your enthusiasm and energy will pass on to your clients. These keys to success will help you grow your company and expand your client base.

Dialogues

Dialogue 1   Wanted on the Phone

A: Hello, thank you for calling Bradford and Sons. This is Tracy speaking. How may I help you?

B: Hello. I would like to speak to your director of human resources, Ms. Jenkins, please.

A: Just a moment. I'll check to see if she is at her desk. May I tell her who is calling?

Unit 3 Distant Business Communication

B: This is Bill Burton from Milford Insurance. I'm calling in regards to our meeting next Tuesday.
A: Thank you, Mr. Burton. Can you please hold on for a moment? I'll check to see if she is available.
B: No problem.
(After a while)
A: I'm sorry. Ms. Jenkins is away from her desk. She has already left for lunch. Would you like to leave a message for her?
B: Yes, please have her return my call when she returns to the office. It's best if she can get in touch with me before 3 pm today; she can reach me at my office number, 635-8799.
A: I'm sorry, I didn't quite catch that. Could you please repeat the number?
B: No problem. My office number is 635-8799. Tell her to ask for extension 31.
A: I'm sorry, Mr. Burton. Just to confirm, your name is spelled B-U-R-T-O-N. Is that correct?
B: Yes, and I represent Milford Insurance.
A: I will make sure Ms. Jenkins receives your message and returns your call before 3 pm this afternoon.
B: Thank you very much.

▶ Dialogue 2   About Fax

A: Did you put this morning's faxes on my desk? I'm waiting for some urgent faxes from headquarters. I'm pretty sure they came in last night.
B: Everything that came in off the fax machine last night is all on your desk. But I noticed that some of the faxes came through pretty blurred. Maybe you can take a look at them. If the copy is unreadable, I'll call them and ask them to refax.
A: Yeah, you're going to have to call them and get them to be refaxed. These copies are so dark that I can't make out any of the words.
B: What about that one?
A: This one? This one is so light that I can barely read it. How can that be?
B: You know, I think the fax machine is out of toner. I can change the toner cartridge. That should solve the problem.
A: Yes, but this one will have to be refaxed as well. And look, there are about three pages missing! It looks like the fax machine ate half my important faxes, and the ones that made it through are so blurred or too light. They're unreadable!

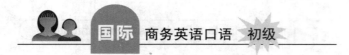

B: I guess the fax machine is out of paper, too. Don't worry. I'll have someone look at it this afternoon, and in the meantime, I'll have your documents refaxed to our other fax machine.

Dialogue 3   Agenda Change by Telephone

A: Hello, Bill Burton speaking. What can I do for you?

B: Hello, Mr. Burton. This is Jenny Jenkins of Bradford and Sons returning your call. I am sorry you missed me when you called my office this morning. My secretary said you called concerning our meeting next Tuesday?

A: Yes, Ms. Jenkins, thank you for returning my call. I am glad to finally get a hold of you. I want to let you know I will not be able to make our meeting next Tuesday. I will be out of town that day. Is there any possibility we can move the meeting to Monday?

B: I'm sorry. I'm afraid I'm completely booked on Monday. Would it be possible to postpone until you return?

A: Oh, dear, I was counting on taking care of our meeting before I leave, but I suppose I could shuffle a few things. Yes, we can arrange something. I will be back Thursday morning. What about Thursday afternoon? Would that work for you?

B: That should be fine. Shall we say about 2 o'clock?

A: Perfect. I'll look forward to seeing you at 2 o'clock next Thursday afternoon. If you need to change the time, please feel free to call me on my cell phone.

B: Thanks, Mr. Bruton. I'll see you on Thursday.

Dialogue 4   Telephone Appointment

(O=Office Assistant, N=Nick, H=Helen)

O: Good morning. Odyssey Promotions. How may I help you?

N: Hello, this is Nick Delwin from Communicon. Could I speak to Helen Turner, please?

O: Just a moment, please. *(To Helen Turner)* I have Nick Delwin on the line for you.

H: Thank you… Hi, Nick. Nice to hear from you. How's the English weather?

N: It's pretty good for the time of year. What's it like in New York?

H: Not good, I'm afraid.

N: That's a pity because I'm planning to come across next week.

Unit 3 Distant Business Communication

H: Really? Well, you'll come by to see us while you're here, I hope.

N: That's what I'm phoning about. I've got a meeting with a customer in Boston on Tuesday of next week. I was hoping we could arrange to meet up either before or after.

H: Great. That would give us a chance to show you the convention centre, and we could also drop in at Caesar's Restaurant where Gregg has arranged your reception.

N: That's what I was thinking.

H: So you said you have to be in Boston on Tuesday? That's the 8th?

N: That's right. Now, I could stop over in New York either on the way in — that would be the Monday… Would that be possible?

H: Ah, I'm afraid I won't be in the office on Monday, and I think Gregg has meetings all day.

N: Uh-h huh, well, the other possibility would be to arrange it after Boston on my way home.

H: When do you plan on leaving Boston?

N: Could be either Tuesday afternoon or Wednesday morning, but I would like to catch a flight back to London on Wednesday evening.

H: OK. Well, it would be best for us if you could fly in on the Wednesday morning. Either Gregg or I will pick you up at the airport, and then we could show you the convention centre and also Caesar's. If there's time, you could come back to the office and we'll run through any of the details that still haven't been finalized.

N: That sounds good. Just as long as I can get back to the airport for my evening flight.

H: No problem. Look, why don't you fax me your information once you've confirmed your flight times? Then we'll get back to you with an itinerary for the day — that's Wednesday, the 9th, right?

N: That's right. Good, well, I'll do that and I look forward to seeing you next week.

H: Same here. See you next week.

N: Right. Goodbye.

H: Bye-bye.

Words and Expressions

available *a.* 可找到的，空闲的，可利用的，可获得的
reach *v.* 找到
blur *v.* 使……模糊不清
toner cartridge 调色块，碳粉匣
shuffle *v.* 推开，推诿
cell phone 手机
drop in 顺便去，顺道去
itinerary *n.* 旅游计划，日程安排

1. 电话问询是贸易中一种很常见的沟通方式。对于生产或交易中遇到的各种问题，如果能通过电话方式解决，那便是最快捷、最有效率的。
2. 在商业领域，通过电话营销，能够使公司的整体工作效率大幅提高。接听电话中需要掌握一些技巧，如注意在接听过程中保持亲切和气的态度、确定来电目的、确定来电者的身份等。
3. 打电话以英语交谈时，只要牢记与善用下列4点就可以畅行无阻。
   (1) Speak clearly.（清楚地说）
   (2) Speak slowly.（不慌不忙地说）
   (3) Don't hesitate to speak.（不踌躇不犹豫地说）
   (4) Write down the message.（把概要记在便条纸上）

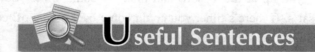

1. ABC corporation. May I help you?
   这里是 ABC 公司，我能帮您什么吗？
2. And you are?
   你是？
3. I'll put her on the phone. Just a second.
   我会请她接电话，请等一下。
4. Would you mind holding for one minute?
   您介意稍微等一分钟吗？
5. He's out for lunch. Would you like to try again an hour later?
   他出去吃午餐了，您要不要一小时后再打来？
6. She is not here but you can call her machine.
   她不在这里，但是您可以打她的电话答录机。
7. I'm interested in your CRM software. Can you give me an quote?
   我对你们的客户关系管理软件有兴趣，能跟我报个价吗？
8. I'd like to place an order for a DL-1100 color printer.
   我想要订购 DL-1100 彩色打印机。

Unit 3 Distant Business Communication

9. I'm calling to check my order status.
   我打电话来查看我订单的状况。
10. I was referred to you by Mr. Gordon.
    我是戈登先生介绍来的。

I Complete the following dialogues.

1. **A:** _____?
   （请问您是哪位？）
   B: This is Miss Li from the United Textiles.
2. **A:** _____?
   （他不在，我可以帮你传话吗？）
   B: No, thanks.

II Situational practice.

The situation: Mr. John Green, our general manager, would like to call Mr. Zhang on June 3 at 2 pm sharp (your time) about the opening of a sample room there.
The task: Create a dialogue according to the situation.

对话汉译

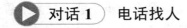 电话找人

A: 您好，感谢您致电布拉德福家庭公司。我是特蕾西，有什么需要我帮忙的吗？
B: 您好，我想找你们的人力资源部主任詹金思小姐通话。
A: 稍等，我去看看她是否在办公室。请问您是哪位？
B: 我是米尔福德保险公司的比尔·伯顿，我想问一下有关下周二我们见面的事。
A: 谢谢你，伯顿先生。请您先等一会儿好吗？我去看看她是否在办公室。
B: 没问题。

（过了一会儿）

A: 非常抱歉，詹金思小姐现在不在办公室。她去吃午饭了。您愿意给她留个口信吗？
B: 好的，请她回办公室后给我来电话。如果今天下午 3 点以前能与我联系的话就再好不过了，打办公室电话 635-8799 就可找到我。
A: 对不起，我没跟上，您能再重复一下电话号码吗？
B: 没问题。我办公室的电话是 635-8799，然后再接 31 分机。
A: 伯顿先生，不好意思。我想确认一下您的名字是 B-U-R-T-O-N 吗？
B: 是的，我是米尔福德保险公司的。
A: 我会把您的口信告诉詹金思小姐，让她在今天下午 3 点以前给您回电话。
B: 非常感谢。

对话 2　有关传真

A: 你把今早的传真放我桌上了吗？我在等总部的紧急传真，我敢肯定昨天晚上这些传真就到了。
B: 昨天晚上传真过来的所有材料我都放在您桌上了。不过，我注意到有些传真发过来的时候就很模糊。也许您可以看看。如果复本不能读的话，我给他们打电话让他们重新发一次。
A: 没错，你去给他们打电话让他们重新发一次。这些复本上的字颜色太黑了，我什么也看不出来。
B: 那份怎么样？
A: 这份吗？这份颜色又太浅了，我根本没法看。怎么会这样呢？
B: 我想，可能是传真机的调色剂出了问题，我可以把调色块更换一下。那样问题就都解决了。
A: 是这样，不过这份还需要再重新发一遍。你来看，还少了 3 页呢！看起来是传真机吃掉了我一半的重要传真文件，而那些发过来的不是太模糊就是太浅，根本没法看。
B: 我猜是传真机没纸了。别担心，我今天下午就去找人来看一下，同时，我让他们把您要的文件重新发到其他传真机上。

对话 3　电话调整安排

A: 您好！我是比尔•伯顿，您有事吗？
B: 您好，伯顿先生。我是布拉弗得家庭公司的詹尼•詹金斯，您给我打过电话。很抱歉您上午往我办公室打电话的时候我不在。我秘书说您找我是要谈关于我们下星期

Unit 3 Distant Business Communication

二见面的事情,是吗?
- **A:** 是的,詹金斯小姐。谢谢您给我回电话。很高兴终于和您联系上了。我想告诉您下星期二我可能没办法赴约,那天我要出城办事。有没有可能把见面时间改到周一呢?
- **B:** 对不起,恐怕我周一的日程已排满了。能否等您回来再说?
- **A:** 噢,天啊,我原来打算在离开之前处理好见面之事,不过我想我可以重新安排一下。没错,我们可以安排一下。我周四上午才回来。那周四下午怎么样?这个时间你可以吗?
- **B:** 应该没问题。我们定在 2 点可以吗?
- **A:** 好极了。我盼着下周四下午 2 点与您见面。您如果要更改时间,请随时打我手机联系。
- **B:** 谢谢,伯顿先生。下周四见。

▶ 对话 4 电话预约

(O=办公室文员,N=尼克,H=海伦)

- **O:** 早上好。这里是奥德赛企划公司。我能为您提供什么帮助吗?
- **N:** 你好,我是国际通讯公司的尼克·戴尔文。可以帮我转接海伦·特纳吗?
- **O:** 请稍等。*(对海伦·特纳说)* 有个叫尼克·戴尔文的人打来电话要找你。
- **H:** 谢谢……你好,尼克。很高兴接到你的电话。英国那边的天气怎么样?
- **N:** 就今年这个时候来讲,还是相当不错的。纽约那边的天气呢?
- **H:** 恐怕不怎么样。
- **N:** 那真糟糕,因为我正打算下星期过去一趟。
- **H:** 真的吗?嗯,我希望你来的时候能顺便过来看看我们,可以吗?
- **N:** 这正是我打电话想要告诉你的事情。下星期二,我要在波士顿会见一个客户。我希望,在那之前或之后我们能找个时间见一下。
- **H:** 太好了。那样我们就有机会带领你参观一下会议中心了,而且我们还可以顺便去凯萨饭店,葛雷格已经在那里为你安排好了接待活动。
- **N:** 我也是这么想的。
- **H:** 嗯,你说你要在星期二的时候到波士顿?那是 8 号吧?
- **N:** 没错。那样的话,我也可以在去之前先去纽约一趟,可能是星期一的时候,那没问题吧?
- **H:** 啊,恐怕星期一的时候我不在办公室,而且我想葛雷格全天都在开会。
- **N:** 嗯嗯,好吧,那另一个可能就是在我从波士顿回来的时候再安排见一下了。
- **H:** 你打算什么时候离开波士顿?

N: 可能是星期二下午，也可能是星期三上午，但我想在星期三晚上搭乘航班返回伦敦。
H: 好。嗯，如果你能在星期三上午飞过来的话，那对我们来说最好不过了。葛雷格或者我可以去机场接你，之后，我们可以带你去参观会议中心和凯萨饭店。如果有时间的话，你可以再去一下我们的办公室，我们可以迅速处理一些还没有解决的细节问题。
N: 听起来不错。只要我能赶回机场搭上我的夜班飞机就行。
H: 没问题。嗯，一旦你确定了你的航班日期，发个传真告诉我具体情况如何？那样我们就可以给你回复当天的日程安排，那天是9号星期三，对吧？
N: 没错。好，嗯，我会的，我期待着下星期和你们见面。
H: 我也是。下星期见。
N: 好。再见。
H: 再见。

Extended Reading

So, if you want to keep and add customers, keep your employees from saying these things on the phone.

1. "That's not our policy."
2. "That's not my department." or "That's not my job."
3. "Could you call back? We're really busy right now."
4. "My computer's down." or "We're having trouble with our servers."
5. "Didn't you get my voice mail?"
6. "I was just waiting to get more information before calling you back."
7. "Hi. Is Pat or Sam or Morgan or Tyler there?"
8. "Wait a sec. I'm putting you on my speakerphone."
9. "I'll see that she calls you."
10. "I just buried my mother."

Topic discussion:

What are the important points in making a business call?

Unit 3 Distant Business Communication

常用词汇和短语

agreement　*n.*　协议，协定
bother　*v.*　麻烦，打扰
cut off　（指电话）通话被中断
draft　*n.*　草稿
follow　*v.*　听懂，领会
hang up/hang on　挂断电话/不挂断电话

hold the line　（打电话时）不挂断
reconnect　*v.*　使重新接通
step out　暂时离开
tie up　（工作等）把……缠住，使无法脱身

Unit

4

Business Appointment
商务约会

Learning Resources

Warming-up

How to Make an Appointment

The most important thing to remember when making appointments is that you are selling the appointment, not your product or service. Therefore, you do not want to be talking too much. You can expand on what you have to offer when you get to the appointment.

1. What you need is your opening statement (something you know about them or a referral).

2. Your "interest-grabbing" sentence, something that offers the customer a major benefit to them.

3. Request the appointment and ensure you give a choice of time so the prospect cannot say "yes" or "no".

Dialogues

Dialogue 1 To Arrange a Meeting

Tony Smith (S) calls the New York Electric Power Equipment Co. He wants to make an appointment with Mr. Hensleigh (H).

H: New York Electric Power Equipment Co., may I help you?
S: Yes, this is Tony Smith. I'd like to speak with Mr. Hensleigh.
H: This is Hensleigh speaking. How are you, Mr. Smith?
S: Fine, thank you. And you?
H: Just fine, thank you.
S: I'm calling to see if we can arrange a meeting. There are several matters I'd like to discuss with you.
H: OK, when would be convenient?
S: Could we meet tomorrow?
H: Yes, that's good. What time would be convenient?

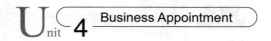

S: How about 2:30 pm?
H: Fine. I'm looking forward to seeing you.
S: Right, see you then.

▶ Dialogue 2   To Make an Appointment

Ifan Merleni (M) of FedEx Corp. calls General Electric Company in order to make an appointment with Mr. Friedberg. However, Mr. Friedberg is out. Melissa Curtis (C), the secretary of Mr. Friedberg answers the phone.

C: Hello, this is Melissa Curtis from General Electric Company.
M: Hi, this is Ifan Merleni of FedEx Corp. Would you please transfer me to Friedberg extension 118?
C: Please hold on, Mr. Merleni. I'll see if Mr. Friedberg is available to take your call. *(After a while)* I'm sorry. Mr. Friedberg is out of the office. Can anyone else assistant you?
M: No, I've got to talk to Mr. Friedberg. It's urgent. When will he be back?
C: I'm afraid he is out for the whole day. Maybe you can make an appointment.
M: Then, well, can I meet Mr. Friedberg tomorrow?
C: Let me check the schedule, tomorrow… that is Monday… Sorry, Mr. Friedberg is busy this Monday; he won't be free until 11 o'clock that day.
M: Then, how about Tuesday? It's really urgent. Your last cargo was damaged.
C: Let me see, how about 10 am on Tuesday? Mr. Friedberg will have two hours free time from 10 am to 12 am.
M: Great.
C: OK, let me check again. Mr. Merleni from FedEx, you want to meet Mr. Friedberg this Tuesday at 10 am to talk about the damaged cargo.
M: That's right. My office number is 9558-1111. You can call me after you confirm this appointment with Mr. Friedberg.
C: OK, I'll inform Mr. Friedberg of this appointment when he's back.
M: Thank you, goodbye.

###

Mr. Friedberg (F) has come back to his office. His secretary Melissa Curtis (C) informs him

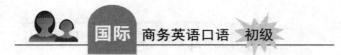

Ifan Merleni from FedEx Corp. called 3 hours ago and fixed a time for this appointment.

C: Hi, Mr. Friedberg, Ifan Merleni from FedEx Corp. called 3 hours ago. He wanted to meet you this Tuesday at 10 am to talk about the damaged cargo.

F: Damaged cargo?

C: Yeah, he said our last cargo was damaged.

F: That's bad. But I have another important appointment with Mr. Johnson from ABN AMRO on Tuesday at 10 am.

C: Oh, then should we change the appointment or cancel the appointment?

F: Change the appointment. We must keep the appointment. It sounds urgent. Would you check my schedule to find some free time?

C: Sure. You are really busy in the following days. You are available only Friday morning.

F: Oh, that's bad. Damaged cargo is really a big issue.

C: Let me check again. En… your schedule is really full during the daytime.

F: OK, can we meet Mr. Merleni at 7 o'clock Tuesday evening?

C: OK, I'll reschedule an appointment with him to see whether he is available on Tuesday evening.

F: Good. Please inform me of his reply as soon as possible.

▶ Dialogue 4   To Arrange New Appointment Time

Melissa Curtis (C) calls Ifan Merleni (M) to inform him of the new appointment time.

C: This is Melissa Curtis from General Electric Company. May I speak with Ifan Merleni?

M: Hello, Miss Curtis, this is Ifan speaking.

C: Hi, Ifan. You called to make an appointment with Mr. Friedberg hours ago. We made a rough plan to meet at Tuesday morning. I'm so sorry to say Mr. Friedberg has an appointment already. I'm afraid we have to change the meeting with you on Tuesday morning.

M: That's disappointing. My issue is really serious. When would we postpone the appointment?

C: He'd like to postpone the meeting to 7 o'clock Tuesday evening. Is it convenient for you?

M: Doing what we gotta do. Well, 7 o'clock Tuesday evening. I'll see Mr. Friedberg at that time.

C: Thank you greatly for your understanding. See you.

M: You are welcome. See you.

Unit 4 Business Appointment

Words and Expressions

make an appointment　约会，预约
confirm an appointment　确定约会
have an appointment with sb.　与某人有个约会
ABN AMRO　荷兰银行
change an appointment　更改约会

cancel an appointment　取消约会
keep an appointment　如期赴约
reschedule an appointment　重新安排约会
postpone/put off an appointment　推迟约会
Doing what we gotta do.　别无他法。

Notes

1. 如何有效地安排约会

（1）配合领导的时间表。文秘人员在为领导安排约会时，要注意配合领导的工作规律和生活习惯。

（2）分清轻重缓急。在领导频繁的约会活动中，要依约会的性质、重要性妥善予以安排。一般来说，重要而紧迫的约会，应安排在最近的时间；重要或紧迫，但不是既重要又紧迫的约会，应酌留时间安排；不甚重要的约会或礼貌性拜访，可适当插入领导的工作空隙中，或者取消。

（3）约会时间留有余地。安排领导的约会时，在时间上一定要留有充分的余地，一是约会时间要错开，每次约见之间留出10～15分钟的机动时间；二是远期安排或答应的约定，时间不能太确定。因时日接近时，往往会因情况有变化而更改约会时间。

（4）适当保密。领导的约会安排，一般要注意保密。给科室和司机的约会日程安排表，内容不能太详细，只有文秘人员自己和领导本人手中的日程表才允许详细。

（5）细致周到。安排约会时，你一定要向对方说明约会的内容、时间是得到领导同意的。特别重要的约会，在接近约会的时间前，应与对方再次联系，以确保约会的顺利进行，并随时提醒你的领导准时赴约。下班前将第二天的约会事项填进小卡片，一张送交领导，一张交给司机，一张自己保存，以供提醒。

2. 约会可采用的几种方式

（1）如果上司告诉秘书，他安排了一个约会，秘书必须把它记在双方的日程表上。

（2）如果通过电话或亲自安排约会，必须得到上司的确认，然后再把它记在双方的日程表上。

（3）如果有人写信查询约会的具体时间，一旦时间已定，必须通知询问的人并且把它记在上司和个人的日程表上。

（4）当上司和某人讨论时，他也许会让秘书安排下一次与那人约会的时间；安排好后，必须确保那人收到书面或口头的通知，并记在双方的日程表上。

（5）秘书或他的上司可以通过信件与外地的参观者安排暂定的约会，这些约会必须用铅笔记入双方的日程表，因为它们可能会有变动。

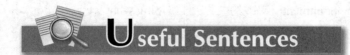

Useful Sentences

1. Will you join us for dinner?
   你和我们一起吃饭好吗？
   Thank you, but I am afraid I've already had another appointment.
   谢谢，不过我已经有了其他的约会。

2. We're just going for a drink. Won't you join us?
   我们刚想出去喝一杯，跟我们一起去吗？
   I'd like to, but...
   我很想去，但是……
   We'd be glad if you could come.
   要是你能来，我们会很高兴的。
   I'm afraid I can't manage it.
   恐怕我没有时间。

3. What are you doing next Monday?
   你下星期一有什么事吗？
   Well, let me see...
   哦，让我想想……

4. I was wondering if we could possibly arrange a meeting for tomorrow sometime.
   我刚刚在想我们能否安排在明天某个时间见面。

5. If you could keep your schedule free on Monday, I'll finalize that appointment with her.
   如果你星期一有空，我会跟她最后落实这一约会。

6. When are you free?
   您什么时候有空？

7. Are you free this Thursday afternoon?

Unit 4　Business Appointment

您这个周四下午有空吗？

8. What time will you be in?
   您什么时候在？

9. What time will you be able to see me?
   您什么时候可以见我？

10. Would Wednesday morning be all right?
    周三上午可以吗？

11. I'd like to make an appointment with Mr. Smith.
    我想约见史密斯先生。

12. I'll call and see you if you like.
    如果您愿意，我想拜访一下您。

13. I shall be free this afternoon.
    我今天下午有空。

14. I shall be here at half past six.
    我六点半在这儿。

15. I'll be very pleased to see you.
    我将非常高兴见到您。

16. I'll be so glad if you can come.
    如果您能来，我将很高兴。

17. I'm not quite sure if I'm free.
    我不肯定是否有空。

18. Monday would be better for me.
    星期一会更好一点。

19. Well, I'm engaged at that time.
    哦，那时我有个约会。

20. I can't keep the appointment because I am sick.
    因为生病所以我不能赴约。

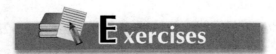

I Complete the following dialogues.

1. **Man:** _____?
   （请问我能和经理通话吗？）

Woman: May I ask who's calling, please?
Man: Tell him it's his friend from California.
Woman: _____.
（请稍等，我看看他在否。）

2. Man: _____?
（你们俩什么时候方便呢？）
Woman: _____?
（下周二或是明天如何？）
Man: Any time except Tuesday afternoon.
Woman: _____.
（我们暂时约定下周二上午9点。）
Man: _____.
（只要您方便，欢迎来访。）
Woman: _____.
（我们真的很期待这次会面。）

II Situational practice.

The situation: Imagine your manager has a business appointment at 10 o'clock. However, your manager doesn't come back to the office and cannot be connected until 9:50. How could you deal with this incident?

The task: Make a dialogue between you and the client.

对话汉译

▶ 对话 1   安排约会时间

托尼·史密斯（S）致电纽约电力设备公司。他想和汉斯雷先生（H）安排一次会面。

H: 这里是纽约电力公司，我能帮您什么忙吗？
S: 是的，我是托尼·史密斯。我想找汉斯雷先生。
H: 我就是汉斯雷。您好吗？斯密斯先生。
S: 很好，谢谢。您呢？
H: 还行，谢谢。

Unit 4　Business Appointment

S: 我打电话是想和您安排一次会面。我有几件事情想和您商讨。
H: 好的，您什么时候方便？
S: 明天好吗？
H: 好的，很不错。您几点方便呢？
S: 下午 2:30 怎样？
H: 好的。期待见到您。
S: 好的，到时见。

▶ 对话 2　预约见面时间

联邦快递的伊凡·梅兰尼（M）致电通用电器公司，想约见弗利伯格先生。但是，弗利伯格先生不在公司，他的秘书蒙丽莎·柯蒂斯（C）接听了电话。

C: 您好，我是通用电器的蒙丽莎·柯蒂斯。
M: 你好，我是联邦快递的伊凡·梅兰尼。能帮我转接弗利伯格先生的 118 分机吗？
C: 请稍等，梅兰尼先生。我看看弗利伯格先生是否有空接电话。（过了一会儿）对不起，弗利伯格先生不在办公室，其他人能帮您吗？
M: 不行，我只能和弗利伯格先生谈。事情很紧急，他什么时候回来呢？
C: 很抱歉，他一天都在外面。您可以预约一下。
M: 好吧，我明天能见弗利伯格先生吗？
C: 我查看下弗利伯格先生的日程，明天……是周一。他周一正忙，要到中午 11 点才有空。
M: 那么周二呢？真的很紧急，你们上批货被损坏了。
C: 我看看，那么周二上午 10 点怎样？弗利伯格先生从 10 点到 12 点有两个小时的时间。
M: 太好了。
C: 好的，我再核对下。联邦快递的梅兰尼先生想在周二上午 10 点约见弗利伯格先生谈损坏货物的事情。
M: 是的。我办公室的电话是 9558-1111。您和弗利伯格先生确认好后请给我打个电话。
C: 好的。弗利伯格先生回来我就确认。
M: 谢谢，再见。

▶ 对话 3　确定约会时间

弗利伯格先生（F）回到办公室。他的秘书蒙丽莎·柯蒂斯（C）告诉他联邦快递的伊凡·梅兰尼三小时前致电预约会面。

C: 您好，弗利伯格先生。联邦快递的伊凡·梅兰尼三小时前找您。他想在下周二上午 10

国际 商务英语口语 初级

点约你谈下损坏的货物的事情。
F: 损坏的货物？
C: 是的，他说我们上批货物损坏了。
F: 有点糟糕。但是我周二上午 10 点和荷兰银行的强生先生有另外一个重要约会。
C: 那么我们是否应该取消和科蒂斯小姐的约会或者改期？
F: 改期吧，要守约。听起来也很紧急。你核对下我的日程看看有没有空闲的时间。
C: 好的。接下来的几天您真的很忙。只有周五上午有空。
F: 哦，太糟糕了。货物损坏真的是件大事。
C: 我再看看。嗯……您白天的日程的确已经满了。
F: 好吧。我可以在周二晚上 7 点约见梅兰尼先生。
C: 好的，我会和他改期看看他周二晚上有没有时间。
F: 好的。尽快告知我他的答复。

对话 4 安排新的约会时间

蒙丽莎·柯蒂斯（C）给伊凡·梅兰尼（M）打电话告知他新的约会时间。

C: 我是通用电器的蒙丽莎·柯蒂斯。我可以和爱若琳·梅兰妮通话吗？
M: 你好，柯蒂斯小姐，我是爱若琳·梅兰妮。
C: 您好，爱若琳。您几个小时前打电话来约见弗利伯格先生。我们之前做的初步的约定为周二上午。我很抱歉，原来他周二上午已经有约了。恐怕你们周二上午的会面不得不改期。
M: 真是失望。我的事真的很严重。我们可以延期到什么时间？
C: 他想推迟到周二晚上 7 点。您那时方便吗？
M: 别无他法了。好吧，周二晚上 7 点，我去见弗利伯格先生。
C: 非常感谢您的理解。再见。
M: 不用谢。再见。

Extended Reading

Prepare for an Appointment with Your Client

Before meeting a client, you should make sure the appointment time, date and place are 100% correct. Some clients would make an appointment with you through telephone call.

46

Unit 4 Business Appointment

If your client can speak good and fluent English and you can listen to him/her clearly, just take a note about the coming appointment. If your client speaks English with an accent that results in unclear communications, you should send him/her an e-mail or a SMS message to confirm all the details on the meetings. And before meeting your clients, you should make clear of what you should discuss about so that you may get everything ready for it, for example, good samples, nice catalogues, detailed technical data on the commodity, prices and etc. And for better achievements in your appointment, you should refer to a dictionary or technical books for some necessary English words or terms about this business appointment.

A good preparation will lead to a good success of the coming transaction.

Topic discussion:

You are a Chinese secretary. Your manger wants to arrange a date with an American client. You must make an appointment with this client. However, this manager have strong accent. You have some trouble in listening. Now, discuss about how to solve this issue.

常用词汇和短语

accountant   n. 会计
air hostess   女乘务员，空姐
applicant   n. 申请人
appoint   v. 任命，约定（时间、地点等）
assistant   n. 助理
attendant   n. 服务员
auditor   n. 查账员，审计员
banker   n. 银行家
barber   n. 为男士理发的理发师
book keeper   记账员
broker   n. 经纪人

businessman   n. 商人
call   v. 打电话
call on   呼吁，约请，拜访
campaign   n. 战役，运动
candidate   n. 求职者，候选人
canteen   n. 食堂，小卖部
canvass   v. 征求意见，劝说
client   n. 委托人，顾客
contract   n. 合同，契约
contractor   n. 承办商，承建人
curriculum vitae（CV） 简历，履历

graphic designer 美术设计员，平面设计师
local public service employee 地方公务员
key puncher 电脑操作员
office girl 女记事员
operator n. 电话接线员
pilot n. 驾驶员
publisher n. 出版人员，出版商
programmer n. 电脑程序员
public servant 公务员
stenographer n. 速记员
system analyst 系统分析员
shorthand typist 速记打字员
saleswoman n. 女店员
simultaneous interpreter 同声译员
tracer n. 绘图员
telephone typist 打字员

Unit 5

Business Agenda
商务活动安排

Learning Resources

Warming-up

- A business agenda is usually written by the secretary and chairperson.
- The best meetings should be scheduled to last no more than two hours.
- Leave space for notes after each item on the agenda.

The meeting agenda is a roadmap for the meeting. It lets participants know where they're headed so they don't get off track. Most importantly, the meeting agenda gives a sense of purpose and direction to the meeting.

Dialogues

Dialogue 1 Start of a Meeting

A working meeting is under process in a famous mobile company in America. (A=Edward Adam, B=Henry Brown)

A: Good morning, everyone. Let us go over the minutes of last month.

B: There are some issues left. Could we continue the item on the agenda last month?

A: I'm afraid that is not the main point for this meeting.

B: OK, but you have mentioned this. I must tell you my view. To be frank, I'm not satisfied with the decision we made last time.

A: OK. You can express your ideas.

B: Thank you. Well, let me put it in this way. I am afraid that our advertisement made for Chinese won't succeed under the present market. Advertisement marketers and analysts say the youth in China has already changed their consumptive ideas from seeking for brands to fashion.
  ...

A: I agree with you to a certain degree, but this is a big problem which should be discussed further. We can make another meeting for this. I think we are getting side-tracked. Let's go back to the agenda today. I'd like Miss Yang to record the minutes of this meeting.

B: OK. Let us move on to the topic for today.

Unit 5 Business Agenda

A: Attention! Today's agenda is how to improve our working efficiency and reduce the expenses. Perhaps we should call our meeting to order. Before we start I hope the meeting will succeed.

▶ Dialogue 2   Discussion on Business Meeting

Anne (A), Henry (H), Cecilia (C) and David (D) are discussing on business meeting.

A: It's half past nine. May we move on to the introductions and the agenda then, please?
All: Right.
C: Well, on the question of improving our working efficiency and financial control, it seems very important to our company. I propose to introduce flexible working hours. Jane, you will be the precise writer.
H: Flexible working hours? It sounds good. How to perform?
C: It means we use a flexible working system. It isn't necessary for everyone to work from nine to five. What's more, they do not necessarily work together.
A: Sounds good. But, how to connect to the topic we discuss today?
C: On one hand, if people can choose working time that are suitable for their own habits, it will be useful to improve our working efficiency. On the other hand, if we let people choose the working time by themselves, it means that even if they work overtime at night, it's caused by themselves. We do not need to pay them call-back-pay.
H: It's really interesting. But I doubt the result.
C: Look, I'd just like to say that we can have a try in some departments.
A: Sorry to interrupt. It's really hard to make decision now. Perhaps we would return to your point later on. Any other proposals?
D: How about using excitation mechanism?
A: You mean?
D: Organizational circumstance is changing greatly. Managerial focus is not to control employees, but to motivate their working creativity and enthusiasm. Through the performance evaluation and efficient communication, performance evaluation system can inspire employee's work enthusiasm and develop employee's potential.
A: I agree entirely with your view. So how about others?
All: Agree.
A: Well, any other points?

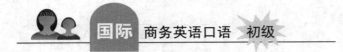

All: No.

A: If nobody has anything to add, Jane, you will give me a detailed plan later.

Dialogue 3 Arrangement for Business Agenda

Anne (A), Henry (H) and David (D) are arranging for business agenda.

A: Perhaps we'd better get started to business. First, we have the introductions and the agenda. Second, I talk about the background, company growth and return on investment. Third, Henry, you talk about the product range.

H: How could I do this part?

A: At this stage we need to present a broad company profile. Don't give too many details about specific products.

H: OK. I'll describe the range and say which products are successful.

A: Good. Mr. Wang may want to discuss certain products, so be ready for that.

H: Well, at the end of this section of the presentation I will ask Mr. Wang if he has any questions.

D: Should we discuss the research and development at this stage?

A: We won't. That will come at the end. Then David, you talk about major markets and sales strategy.

D: Is everything ready?

A: Everything is ready and rehearsed.

D: Right, the product title goes here... Just remind me, is the product called Small Smart or The Small Smart?

A: Small Smart.

D: OK. These letters? Or these black letters?

A: No, I don't like those letters.

D: OK. These letter?

A: Can they be larger?

D: Yes. Like this. It looks good like that.

A: Excellent. It's very clear. It's easy to read. That's what I want.

Unit 5 Business Agenda

▶ **Dialogue 4**   **Discussing Agenda with Secretary**

Mr. Wang (W) and his secretary Susan (S) are discussing his agenda.

S: Good morning, Mr. Wang. Did you have a good sleep last night?
W: Yes, I had a sound sleep. I feel myself fully recovered from the journey.
S: I've drawn up a time schedule for the next two days. Will you have a look?
W: *(Going over the schedule)* Mm, yes. The plan fits me very nicely.
S: You see, I've arranged a free afternoon for you, in case you'd like to go sightseeing around the town.
W: Good. But do we have enough time for our talks?
S: Of course. Do you have any other opinions on this schedule?
W: I'm too busy right now. Put it in my office, would you please? I'll add it to my PIM's To-Do list.
S: Yes, sir. Sally Jones from photography wants to discuss the sports campaign.
W: Hmm, yes, that's a key issue we still have to resolve. What's my schedule like?
S: The earliest time available is in three days.
W: OK, make an appointment with her. We'll discuss the final details.
S: According to your plan, you want to check on the Sunshine Project today.
W: No need. The plan is available. Let us move on to the agenda for this meeting, please.
S: Right here, sir.

Words and Expressions

working meeting　例会
minute　*n.*　记录，会议纪要
item on the agenda　议程项目
introductions and the agenda
　　介绍和会议议程
precise writer　记录（员）
proposal　*n.*　提议
excitation mechanism　激励机制

managerial　*a.*　管理的
evaluation　*n.*　评估
profile　*n.*　简介
presentation　*n.*　陈述
draw up　草拟
go sightseeing　观光
PIM（personal information management）
　　个人信息管理

安排商务活动需注意的文化差异

由于文化背景不同，各国的时间观念也不尽相同。因此，了解访问国家工作时间及假日情况，对恰当地安排商务活动日程、顺利地开展业务十分必要。

每周工作日不同。多数国家的工作日是周一至周五或周一至周六。但由于宗教原因，以色列的工作日是周日至周五，因为星期六是犹太教的安息日，这一天是全国法定休息日；多数阿拉伯国家的工作日是从星期六到星期四，因为穆斯林的休息日是星期五。

回避节假日。例如穆斯林在斋月时的工作日程安排较宽松，这时与之谈生意万万不可操之过急。欧洲人十分重视节假日，每年都会有四至五周的休假时间，尤其是法国人常在炎热的七八月份外出度假旅游，如果这时打扰他们或打乱他们的度假安排，会令对方非常恼火。有些节假日的时间并不固定，比如斋月、复活节等同中国的春节一样，每年的公历日期都不相同，应尽量避开在这些日子里进行商务活动。

上下班时间各异。大致来说，美国人的工作时间一般为 8:30 至 16:30 或 9:00 至 17:00。中午有半小时至一小时的午餐时间。韩国人的工作时间是从 9:00 至 18:00。意大利人从每天早上 9:00 工作到晚上 8:00，其中下午 1:00 至 4:00 为午餐时间。在欧洲上班时要全身心投入，但超时工作却不可取。在日本和中国的香港则相反，人们工作起来不分昼夜。日本的工作时间虽然规定为 9:00 至 17:00，但为了生意上的成功加班加点也是家常便饭。

守时与不守时。对多数欧洲人和美国人来说，让别人等候是不礼貌的行为，即使你的客户迟到，你也应按时赴约。而有些国家对此就不大在意。俄罗斯人在时间安排上就比较随心所欲。在中南美洲以及一些中东国家，预约也都是大概时间，按约定时间前往，你常常要等上一个小时甚至更长的时间。对阿拉伯人来说，工作远不如家庭、朋友及宗教来得重要，他们对时间的感觉是"看上帝的安排"。亚洲人很守时，他们常常会比约定时间提前几分钟到场，但菲律宾人经常迟到。

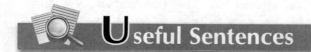

1. What's on the agenda for tomorrow's meeting?
   日程上明天是什么会？

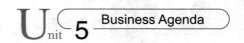

2. Could you please call and remind the attendees before the meeting?
   能在开会前打电话提醒参会者吗？
3. If we are all here, let's get started.
   到齐了，就开始吧。
4. I'd like to extend warm welcome to Reid Edison.
   我想对里德·爱迪生的到来表示热烈的欢迎。
5. We are here today to discuss about what to do next.
   我们今天到此讨论接下来该怎么做。
6. It's an all-hands meeting.
   这是全体大会。
7. Please notify everyone the meeting is cancelled.
   请告知每个人会议取消了。
8. Let's go over the minutes of last Friday's meeting.
   先回顾一下上周五的会议记录。
9. Middy, would you mind taking notes today?
   米蒂，今天你做记录好吗？
10. Kathy, would you like to kick off?
    凯蒂，从你开始好吗？
11. Who is going to write the meeting minutes?
    谁将写会议记录？
12. Keep to the point please.
    请切题。
13. Excuse me for interrupting.
    抱歉，我打断了。
14. I never thought about it that way before.
    我从没这样想过。
15. I totally agree with you.
    我完全同意。
16. Unfortunately, I see it differently.
    不巧，我是从另外一个角度看的。
17. Let's move on to the next item.
    我们继续下一个项目。
18. Are there any more comments?
    还有什么要说的吗？
19. Before we close today's meeting, let me just summarize the main points.

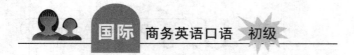

在结束今天的会议前,我先总结下要点。

20. If you have any questions, just send me an e-mail. Thank you all for attending.
    如果你们有疑问,发邮件给我。感谢你们的参与。

I Complete the following dialogues.

1. **A:** We are going to need everybody's input on this project, so _____ _____(我想定下周见面的时间)and hear what you all have to say.

   B: I prefer to meet in the morning. _____
   (我不在办公室)most afternoons this week.

   A: I don't have any problems with that. Let's _____
   _____(那就定在下周三早上九点). We can carry it over to Thursday and Friday if we need to.

   B: Fine with me. _____?
   (其他人有什么想法呢?)

2. **A:** Since both of you have received the copy of the report, _____
   (让我们继续今天的议程). We will have to keep each item to five minutes. Let's start with you Albert.

   B: Our analysis of the research material indicates _____
   _____(工作进行的很好). I have the report right here.

   A: All right, how about you, Paul?

   C: I've contacted the customer. _____
   (他们接受了新的日程).

   A: Good, then I can inform our office to prepare for a new business agenda. Now, _____
   (我们进行下一项议题吧).

II Situational practice.

The situation: You are working in an international business company and responsible for the foreign-related protocol arrangement. Your boss will meet an Israel business partners.

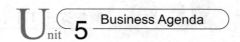

The task: To help your boss to make a business agenda.

对话汉译

对话 1　开始会议

美国一家著名的手机公司正在开例会。(A=爱德华·亚当，B=亨利·布朗)

A: 大家早上好。让我们浏览一下上个月的会议记录。
B: 还有些问题没有解决。我们能继续进行上一次的议程事项吗？
A: 恐怕这不是这次会议的重点。
B: 好的，但是，既然你提到了，我就必须阐明我的观点。坦白地说，我不满意我们上次讨论的结果。
A: 好的，你说吧。
B: 谢谢。那么，我这样讲吧。恐怕在目前的市场下，我们在中国投放的广告不会成功。广告营销人员和分析师认为中国的青年已经改变了消费观，从追求品牌变成追求潮流了。
　　…………
A: 在某种程度上我同意你的观点。这是一个值得讨论的重要问题，我们应该另外再开会讨论。我想我们偏题了，还是回到今天的议程吧。我希望杨小姐做下记录。
B: 好吧。我们就继续今天的议程吧。
A: 注意了！今天的议程是怎样提高我们的工作效率和降低成本。我们按照程序来。在开始之前我预祝会议成功。

对话 2　商务会议上的讨论

安妮（A）、亨利（H）、西西莉亚（C）和大卫（D）正在业务会议上展开讨论。

A: 已经 9:30 了。请大家继续我们的介绍和议程。
All: 好的。
C: 那么，关于怎样提高工作效率和控制财政开支这一问题，我认为对公司非常重要。我提议采用灵活工作时间。简，你做下会议记录。
H: 灵活工作时间？听起来不错。怎样实施呢？
C: 这意味着我们用的是灵活的工作机制。每一位员工不一定要朝九晚五地工作。另外，员工们不一定要一起工作。
A：听起来不错。但是，怎么和我们今天讨论的议题产生关联呢？
C：一方面，如果员工可以根据自己的习惯来选择工作时间，这样肯定可以提高工作效率。另一方面，如果大家自主选择工作时间，就意味着即使他们晚上加班，也是他们自身的原因。我们不必付加班费。
H：听起来不错。真是有趣。不过我对此表示怀疑。
C：注意，我的意思是我们可以在一些部门做下尝试。
A：对不起，要打断你了。现在做决定很难。我们待会儿再谈。还有其他提议吗？
D：激励机制呢？
A：你的意思是什么呢？
D：组织环境正在发生巨大的变化。管理工作的核心不再是控制员工，而是激发他们工作的创造性和热情。通过绩效考评和有效的沟通，绩效考评系统能够激发员工的工作热情，促进员工的潜能开发。
A：我完全同意你的观点。其他人呢？
All：同意。
A：好的，还有其他观点吗？
All：没有了。
A：如果没有其他补充的，请简稍后给我一个详细的计划。

对话 3　安排商务议程

安妮（A）、亨利（H）和大卫（D）正在安排商务议程。

A：或许我们应该开始工作了。首先我们进行介绍和议程安排。其次，我来谈一下背景、公司发展史和投资回报率。第三，亨利，你谈论一下产品的范围。
H：我应该怎么做这一部分呢？
A：这个阶段，我们只需给出大概的公司情况，不用给出太多产品的详细情况。
H：好的，我会描述一下产品范围，说说哪些产品是成功的。
A：好。王先生或许想讨论一下某些产品，要做好准备。
H：好的。这个阶段的演示结束后，我会问王先生是否有问题。
D：这个阶段，我们需要讨论研发问题吗？
A：不需要。我们最后再谈。然后，大卫，你来谈主要的市场和销售策略。
D：一切都准备好了吗？
A：都准备好了，开始排练。
D：对，产品名称在这儿……记得提醒我，产品是叫 Small Smart 还是 The Small Smart？

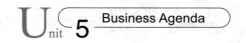

A: Small Smart。
D: 好的，选这些？还是这些黑色的字？
A: 不，我不喜欢那些字。
D: 好的。那这些字呢？
A: 可以大些吗？
D: 可以。像这样的，看起来就很好。
A: 非常好。很清楚。读起来很容易。这正是我想要的。

▶ 对话 4 和秘书讨论日程安排

王先生（W）和秘书苏珊（S）正在谈论他的日程安排。

S: 早上好。王先生，您昨晚睡得好吗？
W: 不错，我休息得很好。我完全从旅途的疲惫中恢复过来了。
S: 我起草了一个接下来两天的日程，您要看看吗？
W: （浏览了一下）嗯，好。这个安排比较适合我。
S: 您看，我们专门为您留了一个下午自由支配，你可以在城里转转。
W: 好的。但是有没有足够的会谈时间？
S: 当然。关于日程，您还有什么其他的建议吗？
W: 我现在太忙了。请把它放在我的办公室里，我会把它加入我的商务通执行表中。
S: 好的。摄影部的萨利·琼斯想和您讨论运动会的事情。
W: 嗯，好，那是一个仍要解决的关键问题。我的日程能安排开吗？
S: 最早在三天后安排。
W: 好，跟她约个时间。我们要谈一下最终的细节问题。
S: 根据您的日程表，您今天要检查一下阳光项目。
W: 不需要了。这个项目可行。我们继续这次开会的议程吧。
S: 好的，先生。

Extended Reading

How to Write Business Agendas

Step 1
Begin by writing the location of the meeting and the time it is scheduled to begin, as well

as an estimated duration time. This will help your members to arrive in a timely manner, as well as give them an idea of how much time to allocate from their schedules.

Step 2

Describe in each heading what is to be addressed, and give one or more possible solutions to the item. This will help facilitate discussion and encourage members to contribute ideas for solutions while at the same time keep the agenda on track.

Step 3

Ensure that each step follows a logical flow, and that you remember to include any topics that were tabled at the previous meeting. Write the initials of the person who was assigned and follow up on old business topics in brackets so the topic can easily be referred to them during the meeting.

Step 4

Indicate the allotted time for each item on the business agenda. Twenty minutes is a good rule of thumb; if an item goes too far over that amount, it can be deferred for following up in the next meeting.

Step 5

Send your agenda to the appropriate persons a couple of days before the meeting, along with any notes or pertinent information. This will give attendees time to think about the points to be covered, thus ensuring more constructive input.

Sample Agenda

Internet Marketing Association Meeting Agenda Start at 10:00 a.m. in Board Room		
Item	Responsible	Time
Opening Remarks	President	5 min
VP Membership Report — intramural report — new member program intro	VPM	20 min
VP Financial Report — status of budget — house bill status	VPF	7 min
VP Rush Report — status of current efforts — status of next-term plans	VPR	7 min
VP Internal	VPI	5 min
VP External	VPE	10 min
Guest Speaker	Community Relations	15 min
End at 11:10 Let's keep on track!		

Unit 5 Business Agenda

Topic discussion:

We will invite President William Taylor and Manager James Horner to Nanjing and Hangzhou in the beginning of May for about 10 days. As requested, design a business agenda for them.

常用词汇和短语

accounts department 会计部，财务部
administration department 行政管理部
advertising agency 广告代理商
advertising department 广告部
assembly plant 装配工厂
background n. 背景
clinic n. 门诊所
customer account department 客户账务部
dispatch v. 调遣
display v. 展出，显示
dispose v. 安排，处理（事务）
dispose of 去掉，清除
distribution n. 分配，分发，分送产品
distribution department 分销部
expenditure n. 花费，支出额
expense n. 费用，支出
expense account 费用账户
financial services department 财务服务部
forwarding company 运输公司
group n. 集团
head office n. 总部
headquarters n. 总部

human resources department 人力资源部
maintenance department 维修部
major markets 主要市场
management department 管理部
marketing department 营销部
packaging department 包装部
personnel department 人事部
product title 产品名称
production department 生产部
public relations department 公关部
purchasing department 采购部
quality control department 质量管理部
research and development department 研发部
sales department 销售部
sales strategy 销售战略
staffing level 人员编制
training department 培训部
wages and salaries department 薪酬部
with a right to vote 有表决权

Unit 6

Business Inquiry and Explanation
商务咨询及说明

Learning Resources

Warming-up

How to Explain Something Clearly

Explaining something clearly can be a challenge to anyone. You need to think about what you want to say and you need to explain it differently depending on whom you are explaining it to.

Step 1 Understand exactly what you want to explain. Make sure you have it clearly in your mind and write down the key points you want to cover. This works whether you are explaining to one person or several people.

Step 2 Know your audience. Explaining a computer program to someone who doesn't understand programming is more difficult than explaining it to someone who does programming.

Step 3 Speak clearly and in simple sentences to explain something clearly. Many people are trying to grasp the concepts you are talking about so you need to make sure you are as clear as possible. It is ideal if you can explain things one on one since you then know exactly whether the person is grasping the point right away and you can change your approach.

Step 4 Get feedbacks as quickly as possible. Again, if you are teaching a class you can have a quiz ready to give right after you have explained the concepts. This will give you an idea of who has understood what you have said and who hasn't and how to continue so you can clearly explain your points. If you are training someone, it is easier to get feedback and know if the person understands you right away.

Step 5 Be prepared to explain clearly by providing examples as well as by speaking.

Dialogues

Dialogue 1 **How to Carry out an Advertisement Evaluation**

Henry Brown (B) invites Joy Wilson (W) to attend an advertisement evaluation meeting and

Unit 6 Business Inquiry and Explanation

tries to explain how to carry out an advertisement evaluation.

B: Good afternoon, Miss Wilson. Did you have a nice weekend?

W: Good afternoon, Mr. Brown. Very nice, thanks. And you?

B: Not bad at all, thank you. We went for a walk on Saturday morning.

W: Well, there is going to be an advertisement evaluation meeting this morning at 9:30. I'd like you to come.

B: I would be glad to come. However, I'm not sure I understand what advertisement evaluation means.

W: Very simply, it's an attempt to decide whether an advertisement is likely to be a good thing for the company to make. Whether it gives a good return on the money or not? Where the market potential is? How long will the advertising effect appear?

B: What does "the advertising effect" mean?

W: When we make an advertisement, we hope some effects would be caused by it. When the audience receives the information, their feelings, thoughts, attitude and behavior would have some changes, thereby enabling the value of advertisement.

B: Who decides whether an advertisement is worth making?

W: We have an advertisement committee. It consists of management service director, sales and marketing director and financial director, who decide whether to drop an advertisement and whether to call out further development.

▶ Dialogue 2 Giving Advice on Personnel Appointments

Tony Smith (S) are seeking advice from Miss Fox (F) about his new personnel appointments.

S: How are you, Miss Fox?

F: Fine, thank you, Mr. Smith. I've studied all your plan, and I think your firm is making big progress.

S: Thank you, Miss Fox. And please call me Tony. Do you have any suggestions on my new plan?

F: OK. First, let's start here. You should set up a separate secretary, clerks, accountants, and cashiers. There's too much work for your people to work in disorder.

S: Yes, they're already overworked. But that will entail more administrative staff, won't it?

F: That's right, Tony. And you'll need at least one group leader for each marketing department.

S: OK, that's a good idea. Miss Fox, what else?

F: En... I think you'll need an assistant to help you deal with some daily work when you are out. What's more, when your business develops, I also suggest setting up another agency abroad.

S: What about personnel there?

F: You'll need the same basic functionality as here. That's all.

S: Thanks for your advice, Miss Fox. It seems like I still need to do some changes on my report.

Dialogue 3 Consulting an Advertising Firm

Edward Adam (A) wants to advertise his products. He is consulting an advertising firm. Henry Brown (B) is an operator, and Lucy (L) is a consultant.

A: Hello! Is this Fly Sky Advertising Firm?

B: Yes, it is. May I help you?

A: Thanks. I'd like to talk with one of your consultants. I want to talk about how to promote our products to the market.

B: OK. I will find a consultant for you right now.

L: Hello. I'm the consultant, Lucy. May I ask what your business is?

A: We are a business computer company. We offer a variety of business computers.

L: Very good! Have you ever thought about advertising in newspapers and magazines, such as *Computer World* or *Businessmen*? You can introduce your products to a special group of readers and attract their attention through many photos and product presentation.

A: I see what you mean, but it's said that advertising on radio is much cheaper. We can save cost.

L: Radios really have some kinds of advertisement. But on one hand, we cannot advertise long time on radio because time is very limited; on the other hand, people seldom listen to the radio nowadays!

A: What about television advertisements?

L: As we all know, among all the advertising media, TV is the most expensive, but it attracts a large number of viewers, especially, the TV product placement.

A: TV product placement?

L: The product placement, also known as product placement marketing, is a different kind of ad from traditional advertisement. It can not exist without programs. It can advertise your

Unit 6 Business Inquiry and Explanation

products in every situation in the TV programs by using the plots, props, characters and scenes.

A: It sounds great!

L: Recent marketing survey shows that people prefer to use this product placement, and their products sell like hotcakes.

A: Maybe I should advertise our products in the TV programs.

L: That makes sense.

▶ Dialogue 4   Consulting Products

Mr. White (W) planned to buy some toys from Ms. Lu's (L) company. He is consulting about products.

L: How do you do, Mr. White?

W: How do you do? It's my pleasure to meet you, Ms. Lu.

L: My pleasure, too. Have a seat, please.

W: Thank you, Ms. Lu. You must have heard of our firm. We are one of the largest toy importers in the world. We used to import toys from Africa and Europe. But now we are thinking of expanding into the Chinese market.

L: That's a piece of good news. We are glad to start business with you.

W: Your exhibits have various goods. Your company seems to handle a great variety of toys. May I know the basic information of your company?

L: We are a specialized toy trading company. In order to provide customers with products of competitive price we have established cooperative relationships with over 100 factories in Zhejiang and Guangdong Province. We can offer many kinds of toys like creative toys, wooden toys, toy cars, toy guns, electric toys, etc. The unit price is ranging from USD 1-100.

W: Thank you. Fantastic!

L: As you know, Chinese toys are highly reputed for their quality and designs. I'm sure they can compete with products from any other countries in the world.

W: May I have a price list, Ms. Lu?

L: Sure, er… but if you have something particular in mind, we could give you an offer.

W: To be frank, a wide variety to choose. May I take the catalogue so that I can examine them further? I'll come back one week later.

L: OK, welcome. Just call the office before you come.
W: Thanks, I will. Good-bye.
L: Good-bye.

Words and Expressions

attempt n. 尝试，努力	consultant n. 咨询员，顾问
market potential 市场潜力	TV product placement 电视植入广告
advertising effect 广告效应	plot n. 剧情
committee n. 委员会	prop n. 道具
financial director 财务总监	scene n. 情景
administrative staff 行政人员	sell like hotcakes 大卖
deal with 处理	exhibit n. 陈列品

怎样接听业务咨询电话

1. 怎样回答求职咨询电话

（1）了解致电人现在的地址。
（2）了解致电人是自己求职还是帮别人求职。
（3）了解致电人现在有没有工作或目前工作岗位。
（4）对致电人咨询的主要内容做出肯定答复。
（5）提出面谈、做进一步人才测评建议。
（6）确定来访与接待的具体时间。

2. 怎样回答劳务合作咨询电话

（1）了解致电人现在的工作岗位及地址。
（2）了解致电人的业务背景。
（3）询问致电人的合作方式。
（4）对致电人所咨询的主要内容做出肯定答复。

Unit 6　Business Inquiry and Explanation

（5）提出面谈或传递双方资料。

（6）计划出下一步业务的具体成效。

3. 怎样接听招聘咨询电话

（1）了解对方的地址及所属行业。

（2）了解招聘岗位及人数。

（3）介绍自己的主要服务内容及服务程序，介绍我们的服务理念。

（4）提出相互传递企业资料的建议。

（5）查阅所传递的企业资料，并做出业务价值及业务取向的分析。

（6）双方签订委托与被委托协议。

4. 接听业务电话的通用模式

（1）热情：具有服务心态。拿起电话在对方说话以前，需要清晰回应及问候对方："您好，××公司。"然后等待对方的下一步回答。

（2）专业：怎样才能专业地回答致电人的咨询呢？首先，我们要了解致电人的咨询内容。一般情况下，致电人会主动向你倾诉，但是，由于说话方式、语言表达、对所咨询业务不专业等问题，致电人在大多情况下，不能完全或彻底地说出咨询的主要内容，所以我们在接咨询电话的同时，往往会有更多的问题向致电人咨询。在双方准确表达出咨询问题之后，接下来，就是做出有针对性的回答。

（3）负责：在一般情况下，对于致电人的主要咨询问题，应以肯定的姿态回答。其实这是一种话术技巧，把具体业务中的一些不确定情况放在面谈或下次业务接洽中而已。

1. There is going to be…
   将要……

2. I'd like you to…
   我想你做……

3. I'm not sure I understand what… means.
   我不太确定是否懂……的意思。

4. Who decides whether a product is worth advertising?
   谁决定产品是否值得打广告？

5. Did you have a nice break?
   您休息得好吗?
6. Would you please tell me what items you are interested in?
   您能告诉我您对什么感兴趣吗?
7. Will it give a good return on the money?
   这是否会收到好的经济回报?
8. We are experienced in…
   我们擅长于……
9. This may take several years.
   这需要几年的时间。
10. What do you specialize in?
    你擅长什么?
11. May I know the line you deal with?
    可以告诉我您做哪行吗?
12. We are keen on…
    我们对……感兴趣。
13. There is a good supply.
    供货充足。
14. Only a small quantity is available.
    库存不多了。
15. The items are in short supply.
    供货紧张。
16. The supply has run out.
    卖光了。
17. We'll keep your requirement in mind.
    我们会按您的要求做的。
18. The licensed product will be hot sales for sure.
    特许产品必将大卖。
19. It is the best seller.
    这是畅销品。

Unit 6 Business Inquiry and Explanation

I Complete the following dialogues.

Susan: Which brand shall I choose?
Lily: _____?
（你喜欢法国品牌吗？）
Susan: Yes, I'd love too.
Lily: Here's a good one. _____
（迪奥以高质量著称）.
Susan: Great! But I heard it is very expensive.
Lily: Yes. _____.
（的确是这样。）
Susan: Well, _____
（我还是想看看其他的）.
Lily: I know another brand _____ （很畅销）. It's not expensive.
Anna: OK. _____. （去看看吧。）
Lily: I am sorry. _____. （没有货了。）

II Situational practice.

The situation: You are a consultant in an air outlet in Shanghai. An American sends a call to book a ticket back to USA after he finishes his World Expo tour. But the ticket he wants to book has been sold out.

The task: How could you solve this problem?

对话汉译

▶ 对话 1 如何实施广告评估

亨利·布朗（B）邀请乔伊·威尔逊（W）参加广告评估会并说明怎样实施广告评估。

B: 下午好，威尔逊小姐。周末愉快吗？

W: 下午好，布朗先生。很好，谢谢。你呢？
B: 还行，谢谢。我们周六下午去散步了。
W: 对了，今天早上9点半有一个广告评估会，我希望你能参加。
B: 我很乐意。但是，我不确定我是否懂得广告评估的意思。
W: 很简单，就是去决定一则广告是否对公司有利并且适合去做。是否收到了良好的经济回报？市场的潜力在哪里？广告效应要多久才会显现出来？
B: "广告效应"是什么意思？
W: 当我们做广告的时候，我们期望能产生一定的效果。当观众接收到信息，他的情感、思想和行为都会发生一些改变，由此广告可产生价值。
B: 那谁决定广告是否值得做呢？
W: 我们有广告委员会。它由管理业务主任、销售市场主任和财务主管构成。他们可以决定什么时候取消广告，什么时候执行进一步推广。

对话 2　人事安排建议

托尼·史密斯（S）正在向福克斯小姐（F）咨询他的新的人事安排。

S: 你好吗，福克斯小姐？
F: 很好，谢谢，史密斯先生。我已经研究过您的计划了，我认为你们公司取得了巨大的进步。
S: 谢谢，福克斯小姐，请叫我托尼。对于我的计划书你有什么建议吗？
F: 好的。首先，我们从这里开始。您应该设立独立的秘书、办事员、会计和出纳。您的员工工作太多又无序。
S: 是的。他们已经超负荷了。但是，这样将会需要更多的行政人员，是吧？
F: 是的，托尼。每个市场部需要至少一名组长。
S: 好的，好主意。福克斯小姐，还有什么建议吗？
F: 嗯，我想您还需要一名助理，在您不在的时候，他也可以帮你处理日常事务。另外，当您的业务发展起来了，我还要建议您在海外再设立一个办事处。
S: 人员安排呢？
F: 和这边一样保持基本功能就好。就这些了。
S: 谢谢你的建议，福克斯小姐。看来我的计划书还要改改。

对话 3　咨询广告公司

爱德华·亚当（A）想为他的产品做广告。他正在向一家广告公司咨询。亨利·布朗（B）是接线员，露西（L）是咨询师。

Unit 6 Business Inquiry and Explanation

A: 你好！请问这是飞天广告公司吗？
B: 是的，有什么可以帮您的吗？
A: 谢谢。我想和你们的顾问谈谈。我想谈谈怎样向市场推广我公司的产品。
B: 好的。我马上为您找一位。
L: 您好！我是顾问露西。请问您做哪一行生意？
A: 我们是一家商务电脑公司，经营各式各样的商务电脑。
L: 很好！你想过在报纸杂志，如《电脑世界》《商人》上刊登广告吗？您可以将你们的产品介绍给特定的读者群，而且还可以用许多插图和产品展示吸引读者。
A: 我懂你的意思，但据说在电台做广告更便宜，可以节约成本。
L: 电台的确有一些广告。但是一方面，电台广告时间有限，我们不能在电台上长时间做广告；另一方面，现在听广播的人很少。
A: 那电视广告如何？
L: 众所周知，在所有的广告媒体中，电视是最昂贵的，但它能吸引大量的观众，尤其是植入广告。
A: 植入广告？
L: 植入广告又称为植入式营销，是一种有别于传统广告的隐性广告。它可以与影视节目相结合，通过情节、道具、人物、环境等进行宣传。
A: 听起来挺不错的！
L: 最近的市场调研表明，很多人喜欢使用植入广告。结果他们的商品卖得很火。
A: 也许我应该在电视节目中打广告。
L: 有道理。

▶ 对话 4 咨询产品

怀特先生（W）计划向陆女士（L）的公司购买一些玩具。他正在咨询产品。

L: 你好，怀特先生。
W: 你好。很荣幸见到你，陆女士。
L: 我也很荣幸。请坐。
W: 谢谢。陆女士，你一定听说过我们公司了。我们是世界上最大的玩具进口商之一。我们以前是从非洲和欧洲进口玩具。但是我们现在准备拓展到中国市场。
L: 这是个好消息啊。我们很乐意和你们做生意。
W: 你们的陈列馆有各种各样的商品。看来你们公司经营各种玩具。我可以了解一下你们公司的基本情况吗？
L: 我们是一个专业的玩具贸易公司。为了能给顾客提供更具有竞争力的价格，我们已经跟浙江和广东的 100 多家生产礼品和玩具的工厂建立了合作关系。我们可以提供多种玩具，比如益智玩具、木质玩具、玩具车、玩具枪、电子玩具等。单价在 1 到 100 美元之间浮动。

W: 谢谢你。很不错！
L: 你知道，中国的玩具是以质量和设计著称。我确信中国的产品可以和世界上任何国家的产品竞争。
W: 陆女士，我可以要一个价目表吗？
L: 当然，嗯，但是如果你有什么特别想问的，我们可以给你报价。
W: 坦诚地说，太多要选择的了。可以给我一个产品类别书让我进一步研究吗？我一周之后再回来。
L: 好的，欢迎。你来之前先电话联系下办公室。
W: 谢谢，我会的。再见。
L: 再见。

Extended Reading

How to Make a Good Impression in Business Talks

Making a good impression on new business contacts is important as it means that the other person will take you seriously from the beginning, and feel comfortable when doing business with you.

Greetings:

How do you greet someone when you first meet them? Do you kiss their cheeks, "air kiss" (kiss the air next to their cheek), hug, squeeze their arms, or shake their hands? The choice of greeting is confusing to many British people who, up until recently, would shake hands in a business context and only kiss close friends or relatives.

Social kissing has become more common in British business culture over the last few years (especially between people who already have a business relationship). However, it is better to give a firm handshake when you meet someone for the first time. This is particularly true when you meet people from cultures where social kissing is not generally practiced.

Introducing yourself: (In order of formality)

— How do you do? (With a falling intonation.) (Correct response is "How do you do?" also with a falling intonation.)

— Pleased to meet you. I'm…

Unit 6 — Business Inquiry and Explanation

— Nice to meet you. I'm…

— Hello. I'm…

— Hi! I'm…

Responding to introductions:

You can generally use the same words as the person who has introduced him or herself. So if someone says "Pleased to meet you. I'm…", you can also say "Pleased to meet you. I'm…". Alternatively, you can just give your name as a reply, but make sure you sound confident, rather than speaking too quietly for the other person to hear.

Introducing others:

Who do you introduce first?

In "Mr. A, I'd like you to meet Mr. B", Mr. A has the higher status. When you are introduced to someone, you can use a standard phrase such as "Pleased to meet you". You don't need to say much at all, unless you are asked a direct question.

As you introduce someone, use your arm to gesture. So if you have Mr. A on your left hand side and you want him to meet Mr. B, move your right forearm slowly away from your body in the direction of Mr. B so that it is clear who you are introducing.

Making small talk:

If you meet someone at a business function, you'll probably spend a couple of minutes in small talk after you introduce yourselves. The topic of small talk is often related to the situation. For example, if you are both at a business conference, the topic of conversation will probably be the conference itself. "Interesting seminars this year" could be the starting point, or "Did you go to the talk by X?" If you are unsure about what to say, take your cue from the other person, responding to their questions, and taking the conversation further.

A: Did you go to the talk by X?

B: Yes, I did. I thought it was really interesting. Are you going to the seminar this afternoon?

A: Interesting seminars this year.

B: Yes, I agree. I particularly liked the one on Asian markets.

When talking to the other party, you should look them in the eye straight. You should look with softness and with interest instead of impolite starting.

Topic discussion:

You are a manager in an international telecommunication firm. You plan to open a new market in China. Now, you are talking with an authority in the field of telecommunication. How will you introduce yourself and your firm to him?

国际 商务英语口语 初级

 常用词汇和短语

apply for　申请
basic wage　基础工资
daily wage　日工资
divisions/departments　n. 部门
extra pay (=premium/bonus)　奖励，奖金
full-time employment/full-time job/full-time work　全职工作
gross wage　全部工资
hourly wage/wage rate per hour　计时工资
manufacture　n. 制造业
maximum wage (=wage ceiling)　最高工资
minimum wage　最低工资
monthly wage　月工资
net/real wage　实际收入，净收入
overtime　n. 加班时间，延长时间
part-time employment/part-time job/part-time work　兼职工作
pay slip　工资单
pay (=wage/salary)　n. 工资
payday　n. 发工资日，付薪日
payment in kind　用实物付酬
payroll　n. 薪水册，工资单
piecework wage　计件工资
press　n. 报业，新闻界
purchaser　n. 采购员

qualification　n. 资格
quality controller　质量管理员
receptionist　n. 接待员
recommend　v. 推荐
redundancy　n. 过剩，多余，累赘
redundant　a. 过剩的，多余的
remuneration　n. 报酬
retailer　n. 零售商
sales rep (representative)　销售代表
salesman　n. 销售员
secretary　n. 秘书
shop assistant　售货员
shopkeeper　n. 店主
skilled worker　技术工人
sliding scale　浮动计算（法），（工资、税收等）按比例增减
staff recruitment　雇员招聘，员工招聘
supervisor　n. 主管人
take on　雇佣，承担（工作），呈现（面貌）
temporary job　临时职业
vacancy　n.（职位）空缺
wage index　工资指数
weekly wage　周工资
wholesaler　n. 批发商
workforce　n. 劳动力
working hours　工作时间

Unit 7

Business Travelling
商务旅游

Learning Resources

Warming-up

It is well known that industrial markets are characterized by extensive personal interaction between a wide variety of functions in both selling and buying companies. When companies establish relationships across national boundaries, the "international variables" of language, culture, education and political differences are added to those present in domestic markets. Thus the need for, and problems of, establishing interpersonal relationships between international marketing and purchasing are likely to be more pronounced.

Business travelling is the practice of people travelling for purposes related to their work. It is a journey caused by business necessities. The place of employment is left temporarily. The business trips have to be approved by the employer, who usually meets the costs. The travelling expenses can be calculated in detail or by a lump sum, depending on the average expense of the destination. It is on the rise especially with foreign business markets opening up.

Dialogues

Dialogue 1 Business Schedules

Mr. Jones (J), marketing manager of a foreign-owned company, is giving instructions about his business trip to his secretary Linda (L).

J: Linda, I'm planning a trip to Chicago and Denver, with Los Angeles as the final destination. I'd like you to make the necessary arrangement for me.

L: Certainly, Mr. Jones. How would you like to go?

J: I'd like to go from here to Chicago by train and spend two days there. Then I'd like to fly to Denver for a stay of two nights. I want to go on to Los Angeles by plane for an indefinite stay of two days.

L: I'll get in touch with the railway station and the airline immediately. Do you still want a bedroom?

J: Yes. And please make sure the train has a club car and a diner.

Unit 7 Business Travelling

L: When do you plan to leave?

J: I expect to depart for Chicago on Monday, September 16th, any time after 12:00 noon. I'll spend the evening of the 16th and all day the 17th there. I'll fly to Denver on July 19th. I plan to leave for Los Angeles on an early morning flight on the 20th. Please book an open return flight from Los Angeles to New York.

L: Will you fly first class as usual, sir? And where shall I make hotel reservation?

J: Yes, first class. I've been quite satisfied with the hotels I've used as lodging before in these cities. Please make reservation for me at those places.

L: Mr. Jones, I have drafted a schedule for your business trip. Would you like to have a look at it? And make some changes if it doesn't suit you.

J: OK. Let me check it out. What a busy day I get on Friday!

L: Yes. You are going to attend the conference in the morning and in the afternoon, you will have to show up on the exhibition.

J: I want to know if I have time for sightseeing.

L: Sure, you have. You get the business down on Friday morning. And you will be free for the next day. You are supposed to fly back here on Sunday.

J: By the way, what's the weather like in Los Angeles?

L: The weather there is a little cold, so you'd better take some outerwear. Maybe you have a chance to see ice sculptures.

J: Fantastic!

 **Dialogue 2** **Getting Through Customs**

(CO=Customs Officer, S=Mr. Smith)

CO: Good afternoon, sir. May I see your passport, please?

S: Of course. Here you are.

CO: What is the purpose of your visit? Business or pleasure?

S: Business. An American corporation has invited me for business talks.

CO: I see. How long will you be staying in the US?

S: Three weeks. I'll be leaving on June 15th.

CO: Where do you intend to visit while in the country?

S: Seattle first, then I'll be heading on to the east coast.

CO: Do you have a return ticket to China?

S: Yes, however, I'll be returning via Japan — not going back to China directly.

CO: May I have a look at your Customs Declaration Form, sir?
S: Well. I've filled in those items listed in the form. Here you are.
CO: Have you got anything to declare? Any gifts for people in this country? Have you got any spirits or tobacco?
S: I've brought some small gifts for friends, and here is a carton of cigarettes I bought on the plane.
CO: One carton of cigarettes is your duty-free allowance. May I have a look at the gifts?
S: Yes... Here they are, under here. I have only a few small gifts — the total value is under $100.
(The customs officer looks inside the case.)
CO: Please open the brown bag. What's in this little container?
S: Oh, that's medicine for my sinus condition.
CO: Could you tell me the ingredients?
S: They are made of herbs.
CO: Herbs? I'm afraid I'll have to ask you to leave them with us for the moment, sir.
S: But why?
CO: I'm sorry, but we'll have to get them examined.
S: Oh, really? This is most inconvenient.
CO: I understand, and I regret the inconvenience, but there's nothing I can do about it. It's the law. We'll let you know our decision as soon as possible. You can close your bag now. And what's this?
S: A box of fruit. It's a gift.
CO: I'm sorry. I'll have to confiscate that. You're not allowed to bring in agricultural products. All right, that's all. Move along, please.

Dialogue 3   Living in the Hotel

Mr. Larkin (L) is checking in the hotel and talking with the receptionist (R).

R: Well, here's your room, Mr. Larkin. I hope you like it.
L: Thank you. Oh, what a nice, large room with a bird's eye view over the city.
R: Yes, all the rooms in our hotel are quite large, and the rooms on this side of the building have a lovely view. Let me open the drapes for you.
L: Oh, thanks a lot. Yes, it's a really wonderful view.
R: The room is away from the noise of the traffic.

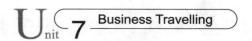

Unit 7 Business Travelling

L: Yes, it's pleasantly quiet here.
R: Here's the bath.
L: Where can we have our laundry done?
R: There's a bag in the bathroom. Just put your laundry in it.
L: Does the hotel run its own laundry service?
R: We do, as most hotels do.
L: I see. Is the telephone on the table good for outside calls?
R: There is a house phone only. But you can ask the operator for city calls.
L: Can I get a city map in the hotel?
R: Yes. Just push the button over there if you need anything. You'll find information about the facilities in your room in the directory, which is next to your telephone. TV is across the room in the corner, and you can find the radio on the nightstand by the bed.
L: Oh, I see, thank you. Now I want to know some information about room service.
R: Oh, yes, you can find the restaurant on the second floor. And the coffee shop is in the lobby. By the way, we have a lot of nice shops and boutiques here near the hotel, so you'll find it easy to do some shopping.
L: Oh, that's very good. Thank you for your thoughtfulness. But is there a hairdresser here?
R: Yes, there's a hairdresser just off the lobby to the right of the desk.
L: Thank you.
R: You can call the front desk directly if you need something like... a taxi or an airport limo.
L: Yes, I see. Well, there is only one thing I want to make sure. When is room service available?
R: Our room service is available twenty-four hours a day. I'm always at your service.
L: Thank you very much.

Dialogue 4   Shopping and Sightseeing

It's the first time for Mr. Green (G) to be in Beijing. Before he leaves for America, his business contact Miss. Zhang (Z) is suggesting some places for him to see and the gift chosen for his daughter.

Z: Is this your first time to Beijing, Mr. Green?
G: Yes. Would you recommend some places for sightseeing?
Z: How about visiting the Great Wall? It is a great attraction for visitors. Someone claimed it was one of the two man-made wonders that could be seen on the moon.

G: That's a good idea. I hear the Great Wall is the focus of the Eight Wonders of the world.
Z: The Great Wall is about fifty kilometers from Beijing — just an hour's trip by car. It lies in the western suburbs of Beijing. When I stand on it, boundless mountains around it come into sight. It's very magnificent. Do you know when it was built?
G: Sorry, I know nothing about it.
Z: It was built in the Qin Dynasty. As a matter of fact, it took a long period in Chinese history. It was built of stones.
G: When and how do we go there?
Z: Let's go there tomorrow by car. Is that OK?
G: Sure. Shall we do some shopping this afternoon?
Z: That sounds like a good idea. Where would you like to go?
G: I'd like to leave that up to you.
Z: I see. Are you looking for something in particular?
G: Yes. I'd like to buy a typical Chinese toy for our little Mary. She is only 4.
Z: I understand. I dare say that you must have noticed that pandas are the pearl of the eye to the Chinese children. China is the panda's homeland. Teddy panda is quite popular with the Chinese children here. How would you like to buy Mary a teddy panda?
G: Great! Just a giant panda for Mary. My daughter will love it.
Z: I'm sure she will.

Words and Expressions

destination   n.   目的地
bedroom   n.   卧铺
club car   设有娱乐室的车厢
diner   n.   餐车
first class   头等舱
reservation   n.   保留，（宾馆房间等）预订
sightseeing   n.   观光
declaration   n.   （纳税品）申报，报告，报关
declare   v.   宣告，声明，报关

duty-free   a.   免税的
container   n.   容器，集装箱
ingredient   n.   成分，因素
confiscate   v.   没收，征用
laundry service   洗衣服务
nightstand   n.   床头柜
lobby   n.   大厅，休息室
thoughtfulness   n.   思虑，慎重
hairdresser   n.   理发师，美容师，美发厅，美容厅

Unit 7 Business Travelling

Notes

1. 出差准备

由于业务需要，上司会经常外出。为保证上司外出顺利，秘书应做好精心的准备。秘书应做好以下事情：准备好外出所需的文件、资料、证件，如护照、签证、身份证等，并准备好一些必备的办公用具。为上司订票和预订酒店时注意细节。在预订机票时应选择飞行时间短、机票便宜但同时又声誉很好的航空公司，这就要求秘书多了解这方面的信息。有的秘书会将订到的机票装进信封，在信封上注明起飞时间、班次和到达时间。订房一般通过酒店的销售部、预订部或前台来预订，有时需要付订金，需通过电话或书面函件确认。预订房间一般根据上司的需要和爱好选择。核实上司前往地的天气情况。如果与上司同行，不仅要做工作上的助手，还要做生活上的助手。如果留在公司里，同样要做好自己承担的各项日常工作。

与平时在公司办公不同，上司在出差过程中的工作节奏更快，对秘书的指示也会相应增多，因此这就要求秘书有更高的工作效率。但是，出差途中的环境毕竟不同于在公司，会有许多不可预见的因素影响秘书的工作，因此既要更细心，又要更灵活。

2. 通关注意事项

飞机抵达外国国境时，必须在最先着陆的机场办理入境手续，在机场接受海关检验。海关一方面检查旅客入境资格，即是否可以入境；另一方面检查旅客的行李是否应交关税，或有违禁物品应予没收。

在免税物品中，包括一些私人物品。对于一些小礼品，若价格低廉则可以免税。对于水果、蔬菜、肉类和肉类制品、活的动物、可能上瘾的烈性药品、麻醉品等，都属于违禁物品，是不允许带入境的。

在入境检查时，照惯例海关官员会问一些问题，这些问题最主要的是确定入境之后的居住地、入境目的及携带钱款等。回答时不必紧张，要针对问题从容回答，如"I will stay at...", "Sightseeing (Business)"或"I have... dollars"等。

在检查行李时要递上证件，如验关人员要求开箱检查，要立刻打开受检，不要迟疑。如果验关人员示意通过，也不要迟疑，立刻提着行李离开。

如果入境后要转机，尽早到要转换的航空公司机场柜台去报到，行李要重新"check in"。如果机场大，不妨询问一下工作人员"Where should I go for the transfer check-in?"。

3. 酒店住宿常识

（1）住酒店对出差者来说是在所难免的。在租住酒店、办理登记手续、寄存物品、结账退房等过程中，酒店都会为顾客提供最便捷的服务。如果有需要，酒店还会为顾客提供房内就餐、洗衣服务、叫醒服务等多项内容。

（2）洗衣服务在许多酒店里都有，在填写洗衣单时，要注意写清姓名、房号，以及送洗日期、送还日期、普通件、快件，并注明件数，以免送错。送洗衣服时还要弄清送还时间，别误了行程。需要注意的是洗衣费不包含在房费内。

（3）房间和浴室内的设备应弄清楚，如有的酒店浴室里除马桶外还有洗涤盆，是专供妇女使用的，不要用来大小便。客房内的牙刷、牙膏、毛巾、浴巾、拖鞋、香皂、纸巾、塑料袋、烟灰缸等日用品，有些日用品需要付费，有些可使用但不能带走。

（4）外国酒店电话可接通总机，如要向酒店外打电话应要外线，打长途电话时，要向总机说清。打酒店内部电话时，可直接拨号。有特殊服务要求时，须先打特定号码，不同国家的酒店有各自具体的说明。除内部电话外，其他电话一般需要另付话费。

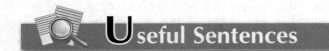

Useful Sentences

1. I'm going on a business trip next week.
   我下周要出差。
2. I have to visit several important clients on this trip.
   这次出差我要拜访几个重要的客户。
3. Mr. Manager, I've had scheduled for your two-day stay in Shanghai. You can make some changes if it does not suit you.
   经理先生，我为您在上海两天的逗留作了安排。如果您觉得不合适的话，可以做些变动。
4. Does my cell phone work overseas?
   我的手机在海外是否也可以用呢？
5. You will go to Shanghai for business next month.
   您下个月要出差去上海。
6. I'd like to book an open return to New York on Flight PA104 leaving this Thursday, please.
   我想订一张不限日期的机票——本周四 PA104 航班返回纽约的。
7. I'd like a round-trip ticket to Tokyo, please.
   我想订一张去东京的双程票。
8. Will you be traveling first class or economy?
   你要头等舱，还是经济舱？
9. One-way or return?
   单程票还是往返票？
10. I need an economy class, open return.
    我要一张不限回期的经济舱往返票。

Unit 7 Business Travelling

11. Do they have any restrictions on what we can take through customs?
    海关对我们携带的物品有限制吗?
12. What are the forbidden items or restricted items?
    哪些是禁止携带或限制携带的物品?
13. Please fill in the declaration form.
    请填一下这份申报表。
14. Are you bringing in anything that must be declared?
    您携带了应申报的物品吗?
15. You don't have to pay duty on personal belongings.
    个人物品不必缴税。
16. Here is your receipt. You're through with the customs formalities.
    这是您的收据。您已办完海关手续了。
17. I'm sorry that the export of these paintings is prohibited.
    对不起,这些画是禁止出口的。
18. I'd like this garment dry-cleaned.
    这件衣服要干洗。
19. Could you bring me an English newspaper please?
    请送一份英文报纸给我好吗?
20. Would you like to have breakfast in your room?
    您要在房间里用早餐吗?
21. Is the telephone on the table good for outside calls?
    桌上的电话能直接拨外线吗?
22. Room service. May I come in?
    客房服务。我可以进来吗?
23. Will it be convenient for you if I come to clean the room in an hour?
    如果1小时以后我来整理您的房间方便吗?

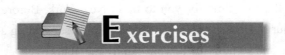

Exercises

I Complete the following dialogues.

1. A: _____.
   (我想把下周的旅行细节过目一下。)
   If you could just bring in the itinerary, and so on, yes?

B: Yes, Mr. Moore, right away.
2. A: _____.
   （这家酒店有没有购物中心？）
   B: No, actually, but the shopping district is not far from there, only ten minutes' walk.
3. A: Mr. Santos, can you recommend a hotel?
   B: Well, _____
   （我极力推荐的是希尔顿饭店）.
   Whenever we have guests, we'll make arrangements for them to stay there.
4. A: What's the purpose of your visit?
   B: _____.
   （我是来经商的。）
   5. A: Right, that's all. You can go through, sir. _____!
   （祝你在这里停留愉快！）
   B: Thank you.
6. A: We'll try to show you as much as possible. _____.
   （我将写出一个初步的游览计划让您先过目。）
   B: Mr. Wang, I really appreciate your help.
7. A: _____?
   （我们先去天安门广场好吗？）
   B: Great! To me, nothing seems better than to visit Tian'anmen Square.

II Situational practice.

1. **The situation:** You are going to make a trip to Chicago. Your secretary Miss Yang has made most of the arrangements, and she is now discussing the schedule with you.

   The task: Create a dialogue about discussion.

2. **The situation:** It's the first time for you to be in New York. Before you leave for China, your business contact person Mr. Jim is suggesting some places for you to see and some gifts for your family members.

   The task: Create a dialogue about your communication.

Unit 7　Business Travelling

对话汉译

对话 1　商旅日程安排

琼斯先生（J）是一家外企的营销经理，正在指示他的秘书琳达（L）安排他的商务行程。

J: 琳达，我要出差到芝加哥、丹佛，最后到洛杉矶，请你给我做一个行程安排。
L: 好的，琼斯先生。您打算怎么去？
J: 我先坐火车到芝加哥，在那儿待两天。然后，我乘飞机去丹佛，在那里待两个晚上，最后乘飞机到洛杉矶，有可能在那儿待两天。
L: 我马上就和火车站和机场的接待员联系。您还是订卧铺票吗？
J: 是的，请确保火车上有休息车厢和餐车。
L: 您打算什么时候走？
J: 周一，也就是 9 月 16 号去芝加哥，中午 12 点以后什么时间都可以出发。16 号晚上和 17 号一天我待在芝加哥。18 号飞往丹佛。19 号我待在丹佛。我计划 20 号早上乘飞机去洛杉矶。请帮我预定一张从洛杉矶到纽约的不限日期的回程票。
L: 您还是订头等舱的票吗？我给您预订哪家酒店？
J: 是的，头等舱。我对这些城市所住过的酒店都很满意。还是预订住过的这几家酒店吧。
L: 琼斯先生，我已经为您的商务旅行做了安排。您想看一下吗？如果有不合适的地方，可以做些变动。
J: 好的，让我看看吧。星期五的安排这么满！
L: 是啊。上午您要参加会议，下午还得出席展会。
J: 我想知道我有没有观光时间。
L: 当然有了。您在星期五上午把生意谈妥，接下来的一天将是您的空闲时间，星期天您将乘飞机返回这里。
J: 对了，那里的天气怎么样？
L: 有点冷，您最好带些外套，或许您能一睹冰雕的风采呢。
J: 太好了。

对话 2　海关通关

（CO=海关官员，S=史密斯先生）

87

CO: 下午好，先生。请出示您的护照好吗？
S: 好，给您。
CO: 您此行的目的是什么？商务还是观光？
S: 商务。一家美国公司邀请我到这儿来谈生意。
CO: 明白。您准备在美国停留多久？
S: 三个星期。我准备6月15号离开。
CO: 停留期间您打算去哪些地方？
S: 先到西雅图，然后再前往东海岸。
CO: 有回中国的返程机票吗？
S: 有，不过回程时我会先经过日本——不是直接回中国。
CO: 先生，可以看看您的海关申报表吗？
S: 好的，我已经填好申报表的所有栏目。给您。
CO: 您有什么东西要申报吗？您带礼物了吗？您带烟酒了吗？
S: 我给朋友带了些小礼物，另外还在飞机上买了一条香烟。
CO: 一条香烟是可以免税的。我可以看一下您带的礼物吗？
S: 行，在这儿，在这下面。只是一些小礼物——总价值不到100美元。
（海关官员查看提包的里面。）
CO: 请打开这个棕色的包。这个小瓶子里装的是什么？
S: 是我治鼻炎过敏的药。
CO: 您可以告诉我药用成分吗？
S: 它们是草药做的。
CO: 草药？我想您得暂时把药留给我们，先生。
S: 为什么？
CO: 对不起，但是我们必须要检查一下这些药品。
S: 哦，真的吗？这太不方便了。
CO: 我能理解，并且为给您带来的麻烦表示道歉，但是我只能这样做。这是规定。我们会尽快通知您我们的决定。您可以合上包了。这是什么？
S: 一箱水果，别人送的。
CO: 对不起，这个得没收。农产品是不准携带入境的。好了，没事了。请过去吧。

对话3　入住宾馆

拉金先生（L）正在入住酒店，并与宾馆接待员（R）进行交谈。

R: 这是您的房间，拉金先生。希望您能喜欢。
L: 谢谢。啊，这是一间宽敞而且能俯瞰全城的好房间。
R: 是的，我们酒店的房间都很大，尤其这边的房间观景更好。我为您拉开窗帘吧。

Unit 7　Business Travelling

L: 哦，谢谢。是的，这里观景的确不错。
R: 这个房间没有交通噪音。
L: 是的，它相当安静。
R: 这里是浴室。
L: 在哪里洗衣服？
R: 在浴室里有个专用袋，把要洗的衣物放在里面就行了。
L: 你们有洗衣服务吗？
R: 和大多数酒店一样，我们提供这样的服务。
L: 我知道了。桌上的电话能直通外线吗？
R: 这是酒店内线电话。但您可以让总机接外线。
L: 我可以在酒店里拿一张城市地图吗？
R: 可以。如果您需要什么，就按那边的按钮。另外，您在客房指南里可以找到怎样使用房屋设施的说明，指南放在电话机旁边。电话机放在房间的角落里，收音机在您床边的床头柜上。
L: 我明白了，谢谢您。现在我想了解一下客房服务的情况。
R: 哦，二楼有一个餐厅，大厅里设有咖啡屋。顺便说一下，饭店附近有许多挺不错的商店，您买东西会很方便。
L: 啊，这太好了，谢谢您周到的服务。再问一下酒店里有美容店吗？
R: 有，美容店就在大厅右侧。
L: 谢谢。
R: 如果您需要出租车或机场交通车，可以直接给前台打电话。
L: 好的，我明白了。哦，还有一件事情我想确认一下。酒店的客房服务时间是什么时候？
R: 我们的客房是二十四小时服务。我愿意随时为您服务。
L: 非常感谢。

▶ 对话 4　购物与观光

格林先生（G）第一次来北京。回美国之前，他的商业伙伴张小姐（Z）建议他去一些地方观光一下，并且给他女儿买点儿礼物。

Z: 格林先生，这是您的首次北京之行吗？
G: 是的。可以推荐几个观光的好去处吗？
Z: 去长城怎么样？长城对游客来说很有吸引力。有人称它是在月球上能看到的两大人工奇迹之一。
G: 好主意。我听说长城是世界八大奇观之焦点。
Z: 从北京去长城约 50 千米的路程，乘车约 1 小时。它位于北京的西郊。站在长城上，不计其数的山脉映入眼帘，非常壮观。你知道它是什么时候修建的吗？
G: 对不起，我对它一无所知。
Z: 它修建于秦朝。实际上，据史料记载，它是历经很多朝代修建而成的。它由石头建成。
G: 我们什么时候出发，怎么去那儿？
Z: 明天我们坐车去吧。怎么样？
G: 就这么定了。今天下午我们去逛街购物，好吗？
Z: 好主意。想去哪儿？
G: 由您决定。
Z: 好的。您是不是想买什么特别的东西？
G: 是啊，我想给女儿小玛丽买一件有代表性的中国玩具，她现在只有4岁。
Z: 我明白了。我敢说您一定了解熊猫在中国是儿童眼里的宝贝，中国是熊猫的故乡。熊猫玩具很受我们中国小孩的喜欢。给玛丽买个熊猫玩具，您看怎么样？
G: 太好了！就给玛丽买个玩具大熊猫。我女儿会喜欢的。
Z: 我相信她一定会喜欢。

Extended Reading

A Business Trip

On a business trip to India, a colleague of mine arrived at the airport in Delhi. He took a taxi to his hotel, where he was greeted by his hospitable Indian host. The cab driver requested the equivalent of eight dollars for the fare, which seemed reasonable, so my friend handed him the money.

But the host grabbed the bills and initiated a verbal assault upon the cabby, calling him a worthless parasite and a disgrace to their country for trying to overcharge visitors. The host threw half the amount at the driver and told him never to return.

As the taxi sped off, the host gave the remaining bills to my colleague and asked him how his trip had been. "Fine," the businessman replied, "until you chased the cab away with my luggage in the trunk."

Topic discussion:

It's the first time for you to be in New York. You are communicating with a driver on a taxi. Then, what kind of topics do you mostly want to talk with the taxi driver?

Unit 7 Business Travelling

常用词汇和短语

订机票:

business class 商务舱
cancellation n. 取消
confirm v. 确定,确认
delay v. 推迟
economy class 经济舱
enquiry n. 询问
flight duration 飞行时间
flight schedule 飞机时刻表
handle v. 处理,操作
layover n. 中途停留

list n. 名单,列表
non-stop a. 中间不停靠任何地方的
one-way ticket 单程机票
reconfirm v. 再次确定,再次确认
reserve v. 预订
return ticket 回程票
round-trip ticket 往返机票
valid a. 有效的

海关:

article n. 物件
contraband n. 违禁品,走私
customs broker 报关行
customs documents 海关文件,海关单据
customs duty (=tariff) 关税
customs invoice 海关发票
declaration for export (=export declaration) 出口申报单
declaration for import (=import declaration) 进口申报单
delivery order 提货单
differential duties 差别关税
drawback n. 退税
dutiable goods 应纳税的货物
duty n. 税
entrance fee 入港手续费

evasion of duty 逃税
excise duty 国内消费税
exempt v. 免税,免除
fine n.&v. 罚款
free goods 免税品
import tariff 进口关税
inspect v. 检查
most favored nation clause 最惠国条款
national tariff 国定税率,自主关税
personal effects 私人用品
preference n. 特惠,优先
scan v. 扫描
security n. 安全
smuggled goods 走私货
stamp duty 印花税
tariff 税则,关税

transit duty　过境税

X-ray machine　X 光机

与酒店相关的词汇：

air-conditioned　*a.* 有空调的
armchair　*n.* 扶手椅
ashtray　*n.* 烟灰缸
balcony　*n.* 阳台
bar　*n.* 酒吧间
basement　*n.* 地下室
bath towel　浴巾
bath tub　浴缸
bathrobe　*n.* 浴衣
bathroom　*n.* 浴室
bayonet-type bulb　卡口灯泡
bedside lamp　床头灯
bedspread　*n.* 床罩
bench　*n.* 板凳
bill　*n.* 账单
billiard room　台球房
booking　*n.* 预订
broom closet　杂物室
built-in wardrobe (=closet)　壁橱
bulb holder　灯头
bulb　*n.* 灯泡
cellar　*n.* 地窖
central heating　中央暖气
pendant lamp (=chandelier)　吊灯
cloakroom　*n.* 寄存处
clothes-hanger　*n.* 衣架
cold and hot water tap　冷热自来水龙头

cotton terry blanket　毛巾被
curtain　*n.* 窗帘
cushion　*n.* 垫子
deluxe　*n.* 豪华的
desk clerk　值班服务员
desk lamp　台灯
dining room/dining hall　餐厅
discount　*n.* 折扣
door mat　门前的擦鞋棕垫
double bed　双人床
double room　双人房
dressing table　梳妆台
easy chair　安乐椅
electric fan　电扇
electric iron　电熨斗
floor lamp　落地灯
fluorescent lamp　日光灯
folding chair　折叠椅
front desk　服务台
frosted bulb　磨砂灯泡
hat rack　帽架
information desk　问询台
lace curtain　挑花窗帘，蕾丝窗帘
ladies' room　女盥洗室
lampshade　*n.* 灯罩
lounge　*n.* 酒店大堂
manager　*n.* 经理
mat　*n.* 席

Unit 7 Business Travelling

mattress　*n.*　褥子
men's room　男盥洗室
mirror　*n.*　镜子
newsstand　*n.*　售报处
opal bulb/opaque bulb　乳白灯泡
peg/hook　*n.*　衣钩
pillow　*n.*　枕头
pillowcase　*n.*　枕套
plug　*n.*　插头
postal service　邮局服务处
quilt　*n.*　棉被
radiator　*n.*　暖气片
register book　旅客登记簿
registration form　登记表
rocking chair　摇椅
room key　房间钥匙
room number　房间号码
rug　*n.*　小地毯
sash window　上下拉动的窗户，框格窗
screen　*n.*　屏，幕，屏风
screw-type bulb　螺口灯泡
sheet　*n.*　床单
shop　*n.*　小卖部
shower bath (=shower)　淋浴
shutters　*n.*　百叶窗
single bed　单人床
single room　单人房
slipper　*n.*　拖鞋
smoking set　烟具
socket　*n.*　插座
sofa/settee　长沙发
sponge　*n.*　海绵
sprinkle-nozzle/(shower) nozzle　*n.*　喷头
stool　*n.*　凳子
suite　*n.*　套房
switch　*n.*　开关
tea table　茶几
thermometer　*n.*　温度计
toilet roll/toilet paper　卫生纸，手纸
toilet/lavatory/washroom　*n.*　卫生间
towel rail/towel rack　毛巾架
towel　*n.*　毛巾
transom (=transom window)　*n.*　气窗
waiter　*n.*　（餐厅）服务员
waitress　*n.*　（餐厅）女服务员
wall lamp　壁灯
wardrobe　*n.*　衣柜
washbasin　*n.*　洗脸盆
waste-paper basket　废纸篓
water closet (WC)　厕所，抽水马桶
wicker chair　藤椅
windowsill　*n.*　窗台

Unit

8

Building up Business Relations

建立商务关系

Learning Resources

Warming-up

Establishing business relations is the first step in a transaction in foreign trade. The development and expansion of a business depends on customers. No transactions can be concluded until contacts have been made between two or more companies. Writing letters to new customers for the establishment of relations is a common practice in business communications. To establish business relations with prospective dealers is one of the vitally important measures either for a newly established firm or an old one that wishes to enlarge its business scope and turnover.

To establish business relations, a firm must, first of all, find out whom it's going to deal with. Detailed information of its counterparts abroad must be obtained. Generally, such information can be obtained through the following channels: banks, chambers of commerce in foreign countries, trade directory, Commercial Counselor's Office in foreign countries, business houses of the same trade, advertisements, trade shows, or even old customers.

Having obtained such information as the desired names and addresses of the prospective customers from any of the above sources, the firm may start sending letters or circulars to tell him how his name is known, the wish to establish business relations, lines of business and the firm's references. Any letter of this nature must be concise and courteous so as to create goodwill and leave a good impression on the reader.

Dialogues

Dialogue 1 At the Trade Fair

Mr. White (W) meets Ms. Li (L) at the trade fair.

W: Good morning. My name is Alan White. Here's my card.
L: Thank you. My name is Li Lei, and here's my card.

Unit 8 Building up Business Relations

W: Nice to meet you, Ms. Li.
L: Nice to meet you, too. Would you like something to drink, coffee or tea?
W: A cup of tea, please. I like Chinese green tea.
L: This is Longjing Tea, famous green tea produced in Hangzhou.
W: Oh, I've heard about it. Thank you. How crowded with the people!
L: Yes, many visitors come to the Fair every year.
W: It's held once a year, right?
L: Yes. The Fair has become very important in our foreign trade. There are many new products on display. Visitors can see samples of what there is to buy.
W: You can sit down to have a business talk with the seller in his booth and buy something you like.
L: Many Chinese foreign trade companies come here and do both import and export business here. Is this your first visit to the Fair?
W: That's right. And also my first visit to China. The purpose of my visit to the Fair is to establish business relations with some Chinese companies in our business line.
L: I'm so delighted to have made your acquaintance, Mr. White. May I know the main products you traded in?
W: I'm in the leather products.
L: I see. Would you be interested in seeing the leather bags? They are made by our company.
W: Thanks, they are rather attractive, but I think there is nothing better than seeing things in actual operation.
L: Yes, of course. Would you like to make an inspection tour of some factories?
W: Yes, very much, if it wouldn't add inconvenience to you. First-hand information is always more valuable than reading pamphlets.
L: I'll make the arrangement and let you know the time tomorrow.
W: That would be great.

▶ Dialogue 2   Making Business Contact

Having done some lucrative business at Guangzhou Trade Fair, Mr. Jackson (J) is pleased to come to Shanghai for the establishment of business relations with Ms. Sun Min (S), sales manager of Inter Trading Co.

J: Good morning. My name is Bennet Jackson, import manager of DB Trading Company in New York. Here is my business card. The purpose of my coming here is to establish business relations with you.

S: Oh, that's good. These days I have met so many businessmen from abroad, who are willing to enter into business relations with us.

J: Ms. Sun, we have done some lucrative business at the Guangzhou Trade Fair. Having compared goods made in your country with those of others, we found yours are satisfactory. What impressed me most is the quality and price. Your products have obtained unanimous approval in the international market.

S: Thank you for saying so.

J: So we are willing to establish long-term business relations with you.

S: Your desire coincides with ours. You have rich experience in marketing and a large number of customers. It's very beneficial for us to establish long-term business relations with you.

J: While you have the advanced technology, personnel and expertise in serving the needs of the market, it's helpful for us to develop new market.

S: We are sure that the business between us will be greatly expanded in the years to come. What do you intend to purchase from us this time?

J: Our company is specializing in textiles. Through the courtesy of the Commercial Counselor's Office of the American Embassy in Beijing, we have learned that you specialize in export business of textiles, and you have enjoyed the highest reputation in the commercial circles.

S: It's very nice of you to say so. It's our principle to do business with others according to the international practice. Our textile products have been exported to more than 100 countries and regions, and have been enjoying great popularity and selling well.

J: Yeah, purchasers say that the quality and variety of your textile products are very attractive. That's why I come to talk with you.

S: As for establishing business relations, we'll be glad to do whatever we can.

J: Ms. Sun, although our company is a newly established one, we have a good financial position. Here is the address and contacts of our banker.

S: Thank you.

Dialogue 3   A Visit to the Sample Room

Mr. David (D) from the Canada is visiting the sample room of a foodstuffs import & export company. Ms. Wang (W), the sales manager of the company, is accompanying him.

Unit 8 Building up Business Relations

W: Here is our sample room.

D: You certainly have got a large collection of sample food here.

W: Yes. We are exporting a wide range of food to many countries. And the demand is getting greater and greater.

D: So it is. Though we haven't done business with you, as you know, your exports of food to our country have considerably increased during the last few years. It appears that Chinese food is very attractive.

W: You said it. The quality of ours is as good as that of many other suppliers, while our prices are not as high as theirs. By the way, which items are you interested in?

D: Canned goods are of special interest to me, particularly the canned fruit and meat. As your canned fruit is among the most popular ones in our market, I'm going to place an order in a day or two.

W: Good. How about our canned meat?

D: I think it will also find a good market in our country. Will you show me some samples?

W: Yes. This way, please. Our canned meat is in various weights. The largest one weighs four and a half pounds net, and the smallest seven ounces net.

D: The small sizes are more saleable in our market than the large ones. I've brought with me a sample of canned meat, which is only six ounces. The smallest size of yours is even bigger than that of mine. I wonder if your canned meat tastes better.

W: You are welcome to have a try. Here it is. Ours is of prime quality.

D: Oh, it's delicious. Mm... I'm not sure about the pesticide residues in your foodstuffs. I'm sure you must have given much thought to the matter. But you know, our government restrictions have been getting more and more tight, so we are not allowed to import any polluted goods.

W: You can rest assured. Our foodstuffs are guaranteed to conform to the WHO standards.

D: Good. I'd like to order meat of this kind in seven ounce tins if the price is competitive.

W: What about other canned goods, such as canned mushrooms and vegetables?

D: They are not as saleable as canned fruit, I suppose.

W: Mm, no, I really don't think so. They are also among our major exports and have found a favorable reception in many other countries.

D: Then, may I have a look at the samples first?

W: Certainly. Here you are.

D: Ah, very nice indeed. But I am not sure whether they are to the taste of our people. May I take some samples home before I make a decision?

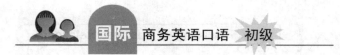

W: That's all right.
D: Ms. Wang, I am really impressed by your products.
W: Thank you. Well, I have an appointment at 5:00. Shall we talk the details over tomorrow afternoon?
D: OK. See you tomorrow.
W: Goodbye.

Dialogue 4   Discussing the Details

Ms. Brown (B) comes to visit a Chinese trading company to discuss the possibility of importing some products with Mr. Chen (C).

B: Hello, Mr. Chen.
C: Hello, Ms. Brown, glad to see you again.
B: I'm very interested in your products, and would like to discuss with you the possibility of importing some products.
C: Ms. Brown, we appreciate your interest in our company very much. My firm has wide business relations with many corporations in your country. Every year, we export a lot of our products to European countries, but yours seems quite new to us.
B: Well, we work for leather products only for several years, but we are in a position to place large orders with competitive suppliers. This time, we are desirous to see the possibilities of switching our purchase to you.
C: That's fine. Our leather bags have enjoyed a high reputation in the European market. Have you got anything in mind you're interested in?
B: Well, I find article No. 338 rather attractive.
C: It's our newly designed one. Compared with the old ones, it is much better in style. Reports from different markets show that this model is the choice of discriminating buyers.
B: You know, Mr. Chen, quality is as much important as the price.
C: Yes. This style is an improvement upon the old styles in many respects. We pay much attention to not only its quality but also its cost. After studying our samples and price list, I'm sure you will be satisfied.
B: So you really don't see your way to get it down a bit? If you come down to the old price, we can place an order of a large quantity.
C: I'm sorry, Ms. Brown. This is our rock-bottom price. When I fixed with you last time, I told

Unit 8 Building up Business Relations

you repeatedly that it was for the trial order only, just to help you get a start. That's an exceptional case. We can't close any more business on the same basis, to say nothing of making reductions. If you find it unworkable, we have no other choice but to call the deal off.

Words and Expressions

business card	名片	international practice	国际惯例
lucrative	a. 获利的	variety	n. 品种
unanimous approval	一致的赞同	accompany	v. 伴随，陪伴
long-term business relations	长期的业务关系	pesticide	n. 农药
coincide with	与……相符	residue	n. 残余，剩余，渣滓
beneficial	a. 有益的	foodstuff	n. 粮食，食品
expertise	n. 专业知识	guarantee	v. 保证
specialize in	专营	mushroom	n. 蘑菇
textile	n. 纺织品	appreciate	v. 感激
through the courtesy of	经……的介绍	rock-bottom	a. 最低的，最低水平的，最低限度的

Notes

1. 建立商贸关系

贸易的第一步就是确定市场和客户。在国际贸易中，进口商与出口商地处不同的国家或地区，相距千里，了解对方的情况非常不容易。以下渠道可使进出口商相互了解：

银行可以提供有关当地进出口商的资料，如公司名称和地址等。

西方国家几乎每个城市都有商会（chambers of commerce）。商会成员就是当地的商人和企业主等。商会的主要作用就是搜集信息和为其成员介绍新的业务机会。

在中国驻国外商务参赞处（commercial counselor's office）可获得有关商业资料。

贸易行名录（trade directory）。

广告。国内外的报刊、广播电视等都刊登大量的广告，从中能获得大量信息，发现潜在客户。

交易会和展销会。我国每年都定期举办交易会，如广交会、华交会，还有国外的展销会等。会上往往有大量的外商。这是一个了解结识外商最直接的有效途径。也可以经商界朋友介绍结识新公司。

互联网。在"信息时代"的今天，互联网为我们提供了大量的信息。商务人员可以从网上获得贸易机会，结识客户。互联网是近年发展起来的新的贸易渠道，在商务领域发展迅速，深受欢迎。

获得外商的资料后，可以通过信件、传真、电子邮件、电话等方式与对方直接联系，建立贸易关系。也可以直接到对方公司或企业，亲自了解客户的有关情况，从而获得亲身体验。

在介绍公司和产品时可以利用目录、小册子、公司简介和结算表来明示商品的优良品质和特色，并详细说明交易条件和交易内容，列出供查询信用的公司厂商名称，并且也希望对方提供同类资料，供己方参考。

2. 中国进出口商品交易会

（1）中国进出口商品交易会（简称"广交会"）每年在广州市举办两次。

（2）在广交会上，许多外国商人与中国出口商进行洽谈。他们签订大量的合同。外国商人说，中国出口的商品质量好、价格公道。

（3）中国的对外开放政策使广交会更为丰富多彩，更为成功。来样订货和不同的支付方式都可接受，这种变化深受外国朋友的欢迎。

（4）中国的出口公司正在竭尽全力改进出口商品的质量、设计、包装和交货方式，以使出口商品在海外市场更具竞争力。

3. 参展注意事项

（1）要充分利用展览会的时机，多接触参展商。

（2）除与客户洽谈业务外，应保持站立姿态。

（3）在展位内，不应该看闲书与报刊。

（4）在展会上应杜绝随意吃喝现象。

（5）关注与发现每一个潜在客户是参展商的重要目标。

（6）参展期间，要注意接听手机的方式和时间。

（7）展会上发放宣传资料，注意合适的方法。

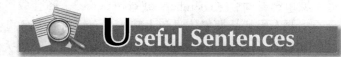

Useful Sentences

1. The quality is superior, yet the price is very reasonable.
   我们的产品物美价廉。
2. This is this year's latest design. It's sold remarkably fast during the domestic trial sale

Unit 8 Building up Business Relations

period.

这是今年最新的设计。在国内试销期间，销路相当得好。

3. I'm glad to have the opportunity to recommend to you our latest laser and electronic product of this year.

   我很荣幸有机会向您介绍本年度最新型的激光电子产品。

4. I got your name and address from the Commercial Counselor's Office of the Chinese Embassy here.

   我从驻这里的中国大使馆商务参赞处得知了贵公司的名称和地址。

5. I have little information about your product.

   我对你们的产品知道的不多。

6. Are they available for export for the time being?

   不知现在是否可供出口？

7. We can produce goods modeled after the fashion of different markets. Of course, we can produce shoes modeled after your samples.

   我们能按不同市场的流行款式制作不同的产品。当然，我们也可以按贵方样品鞋生产产品。

8. I'm sure our business dealings will develop quickly and productively.

   我可以肯定我们之间的业务关系会发展得既快又富有成效。

9. We always adhere to the principle of equality and mutual benefit.

   我们一向遵从平等互利的原则。

10. I'd like to negotiate with you about the leather crafts.

    我想和你们商谈皮革制品方面的业务。

11. The purpose of my coming here is to discuss the possibility of importing into the United States a number of your products.

    我特地来与你们商谈向美国进口贵公司某些产品的可能性。

12. I can send you a price list and a brochure of this series for your reference.

    我可以寄给您一份价目表和商品手册，以供参考。

13. These products are of great interest to us.

    我们对这些产品非常感兴趣。

14. You're recommended to us by a reliable friend.

    我们的一位可信赖的朋友把贵公司介绍给我们。

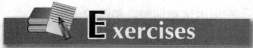

Exercises

I Complete the following dialogues.

1. A: What can I do for you?
   B: We are a big supplier for the Northeast market here. _____
   _____.
   （我想我们两家公司会有一些业务往来。）

2. A: How much do you know about our product? Do you have anything you are particularly interested in?
   B: Actually I have little information about your product. _____
   _____.
   （如果您能寄送商品目录和小册子，我将不胜感激。）

3. A: Would you tell me whom I should contact then?
   B: Yes. Yonghe Trading Company represents us in your regions. _____
   _____.
   （你可以和那儿的销售经理张先生联系。）

4. A: Good afternoon, Miss. _____?
   （您对什么产品特别感兴趣呢？）
   B: I'm interested in telephones.

5. A: _____?
   （我能看看样品吗？）
   B: Of course, wait a minute, please.

6. A: Thank you for your information. _____
   （双方建立业务关系是互利的。）I have no doubt that it will bring about benefit between us.
   B: So do I.

II Situational practice.

1. **The situation:** Imagine you are one of the leading importers of electronic products in your city. You are now having a talk on the possibility of entering into business relations with a Japanese exporter.
   The task: Create a dialogue about the communication.

2. **The situation:** You are meeting a prospective buyer from Australia at the trade fair who is

Unit 8 Building up Business Relations

looking for certain products that you can export. He is comparing similar products in the Chinese market.

The task: Try to give him a comprehensive introduction of your company and products.

对话汉译

对话 1 参加贸易展会

怀特先生（W）与李女士（L）在贸易展会上相遇。

W: 早上好。我叫阿兰·怀特，这是我的名片。
L: 谢谢。我叫李蕾，这是我的名片。
W: 很高兴见到你，李女士。
L: 您好。请问您要喝点什么饮品，咖啡还是茶？
W: 来杯茶吧，我喜欢中国的绿茶。
L: 这是著名的西湖龙井绿茶，产地是杭州。
W: 哦，我听说过。谢谢你。这么多人啊！
L: 是的，交易会每年都有很多来宾。
W: 交易会每年举行一次，对吗？
L: 是的。交易会已成为我们对外贸易的重要渠道。展出的新产品非常多，来宾可以看样品订货。
W: 你可以和卖主坐在他的展位里谈生意，买你喜欢的东西。
L: 许多国内的外贸公司都来这里做进出口生意。这是您第一次来参加交易会吗？
W: 是的，这也是我第一次来中国。参加交易会的目的是想跟中国的同行建立商贸关系。
L: 我很高兴在交易会上认识怀特先生。请问您从事哪种行业？
W: 我是做皮制产品的。
L: 我知道了。您有兴趣看看这些皮包吗？它们是我们公司生产的。
W: 谢谢，它们是很吸引人。但是我认为最好能看到实际生产情况。
L: 那当然。您想视察一些工厂吗？
W: 是的，很想，如果不会给你们添麻烦的话。掌握第一手资料总比读一些小册子有价值得多。
L: 我会安排的，明天告诉您具体时间。
W: 那太好了。

对话 2　建立业务关系

杰克逊先生（J）在广交会上做了一些赚钱的生意后，欣然来到上海与英特贸易公司的销售经理孙敏女士（S）建立业务关系。

J: 早上好，我是纽约 DB 贸易公司进口部经理本尼特·杰克逊。这是我的名片。我来此的目的是想与贵方建立业务关系。

S: 啊，太好啦。近几天我会见了许多外国商人，他们都是想与我们建立商业关系的。

J: 孙女士，我们在广交会上做了些赚钱的生意。把贵国商品与其他国家的商品比较后，我们发现贵国商品非常令人满意，给我印象最深的是贵国商品的质量和价格。在国际市场上，贵公司产品广获好评。

S: 感谢您这样说。

J: 因此我们希望与贵方建立长期的业务关系。

S: 贵方的希望与我方是一致的。贵方有丰富的营销经验和广大的客户。对我们来说与贵方建立长期的业务关系是很有利的。

J: 而你们在满足市场需求方面有先进的技术、人员及专业知识。对我们开拓新市场是很有帮助的。

S: 相信你我双方的业务随着时间的推移将会有巨大的拓展。请问，这次您想买什么商品？

J: 我们公司专营纺织品。经美国驻北京大使馆商务参赞处介绍，得知贵公司专门经营纺织品出口业务，而且贵公司在商界有极高的声誉。

S: 谢谢您的夸奖。按照国际惯例与他人做生意是我们的一贯原则。我们的纺织品已出口到一百多个国家和地区，受到普遍欢迎，而且销路很好。

J: 是的，买主们都说，贵公司的纺织品无论是质量还是品种都很具有吸引力。这就是我来此与您商谈的原因。

S: 至于建立商业关系，我们会乐于尽力的。

J: 孙女士，尽管我们公司是一家新建公司，但我们的财务状况良好，这是我们开户行的地址和联系方式。

S: 谢谢。

对话 3　参观样品室

在一家食品进出口公司销售经理王女士（W）的陪同下，来自加拿大的戴维先生（D）正在该公司的样品室参观。

W: 这是我们的样品室。
D: 你们在这里展览了一大批食品样品。

Unit 8 Building up Business Relations

W: 是的。我们向许多国家出口大量的食品,而且需求量越来越大。
D: 您说得对。虽然我们之间没有业务联系,但是知道最近几年,贵公司向我国出口的食品数量大增。这表明中国食品非常有吸引力。
W: 确实如此。我们的产品质量与其他生产商的一样好,而我们的价格却低于他们。顺便问一下,您对哪类产品感兴趣?
D: 我对罐头食品,尤其是水果罐头和肉罐头非常感兴趣。因为贵公司的水果罐头在我国市场上非常畅销,我想一两天之内就下订单。
W: 好的。那么肉罐头呢?
D: 我想它们在我国销路也会很不错的。您能让我看一下样品吗?
W: 可以。这边请。我们的肉罐头重量分许多种,最大的净重 4.5 磅,最小的净重 7 盎司。
D: 在我国,重量小的罐头比重量大的罐头更好销售。我随身带来一个肉罐头的样品,只有 6 盎司重。你们最小的产品比我的还要大。我想知道你们的罐头味道如何。
W: 欢迎您来品尝。给,我们的产品质量是最好的。
D: 哦,好吃极了。嗯……我不太清楚你们的食品中有没有残留的农药,但是我相信你们一定会充分考虑这一点的。您知道,我国政府的规定越来越严格,受污染的食品是严格禁止进口的。
W: 您完全可以放心。我们的食品保证符合世界卫生组织颁布的标准。
D: 好。如果价格有竞争力,我可以订购这种 7 盎司的肉罐头。
W: 那么其他罐头呢?比如蘑菇罐头和蔬菜罐头?
D: 我认为他们不如水果罐头畅销。
W: 嗯,不,我不这么认为。它们也是我们的主要出口产品,而且在其他许多国家都很畅销。
D: 那么,我能先看一下样品吗?
W: 当然可以。请看。
D: 啊,的确非常好。但是我不能确定它们是否适合我国国民的口味。在我做出决定之前,我能带走一些样品吗?
W: 可以。
D: 王女士,贵公司的产品给我留下了非常深刻的印象。
W: 谢谢。嗯,我 5 点钟的时候有个约会。我们明天下午再详细讨论相关的细节好吗?
D: 好的。明天见。
W: 再见。

▶ 对话 4 商谈细节

布朗女士(B)来到中国的一家贸易公司做业务拜访并与陈先生(C)商谈进口产品的可能性。

B: 陈先生,您好。

C: 您好，布朗女士。很高兴再次见到您。
B: 我对你们的产品挺感兴趣的，想和您商谈一下可能进口贵公司某些产品的事情。
C: 布朗夫人，很高兴您对我们的产品有这么浓厚的兴趣。我们公司与你们国家的许多公司都有贸易往来。我们每年都要向欧洲各国出口大量的产品。不过你们公司对于我们来说，还是新客户。
B: 是的。我们做皮具生意的时间不长，只有几年。但是，对于有实力的公司，我们的订货量还是相当可观的。这一次，我们想看看是否有可能在你们公司订货。
C: 很好。我们的皮包在欧洲市场有很好的口碑。您对我们哪些产品感兴趣？
B: 我觉得货号338不错。
C: 这是我们新设计的一个款式。与过去旧式的产品相比，在款式上可以说是一个进步。从市场反馈的情况来看，这个款式是明智买商的首选。
B: 陈先生，我认为，质量和价格同等重要。
C: 是的。这个款式比起旧的款式，在许多方面都有所进步。我们在改进的时候，不仅注意到提高产品的质量，还注意到了降低产品成本。在看过我们的样品和价目单后，我相信您一定会满意的。
B: 您真的不能降一点儿价吗？如果您照原来的价格成交，我们可以订一大批货。
C: 很抱歉，布朗女士。这是我们的最低价。我上次与您定价的时候反复向您说明，原来的价格只是对试订货来说的，只是帮助你们启动生意。这是个例外。我们不能以此价格再次成交，更不用说降低价格。如果你们认为不能接受，我们也没有办法，订单只好取消。

Extended Reading

To Be a Good Conversationalist

Have you ever wished you were better at making conversation? A great conversationalist is someone who connects with people and makes them feel important. When they talk to you, they make you feel like you're the only person in the room.

Becoming a good conversationalist requires knowing three things: **first, how to start a conversation; second, how to keep it going; and third, how to end it.**

Starting a conversation usually means coming up with an opening line or icebreaker. The best kind of icebreaker is one that's positive. The last thing people want to hear from a stranger is how noisy the party is, how awful the food is, or how ugly the people are dressed.

A compliment is always a good icebreaker and will usually be appreciated. Any news

Unit 8 Building up Business Relations

event is a good icebreaker. Read the newspaper because it's so important to know what's going on in the world. The fact is, any opening line will do, as long as it's not negative. The best way to entice a person to have a conversation with you is by being sincere and respectful, and letting them know that you are interested in talking to them.

Once you've got a conversation going, the best way to keep it going is by asking the other person questions that don't require just a *yes* or *no* answer or questions which show genuine interest on your part. For example, if someone says, "*I'm from Miami,*" you may respond with, "*I've been to Miami!*" and continue with, "*How long have you lived there?*" then, "*I was born there, and I've lived there all my life.*" You might say, "*I've never met anyone who is a Florida native. Is your family from Miami as well?*"

You keep asking questions based on the last thing a person says. This is called the "elaboration technique". Choose questions that will get the other person to elaborate on what they're saying. Ask questions similar to those a reporter might ask to draw a person out: who, what, when, where and why questions.

Once you hit on something you find interesting, keep asking questions in order to get the person to elaborate about the topic as much as possible. A good conversationalist elaborates on the experiences they've had. Instead of saying the party was fun, tell why it was fun. Describe why you had a good time—who was there, what happened, where it was, and how people arranged the party. Go into detail. Description is the best form of communication because it keeps people's interest up and stimulates them. Use words to create images and paint pictures so that the other person can get a visual as well as an auditory image of what you're describing to them. If you use the description effectively, you can make the person feel as though they were actually there. Here are seven tips that can help you be an excellent communicator:

Be aware of your own body and facial language. Make a good facial contact when you speak, and be physically expressive without being excessive.

Don't gossip. You run the risk of offending the person you're talking to. It also makes you look small.

Cultivate a wide range of topic.

Have a sense of humor. Everyone enjoys a humorous story or joke. Sexual and ethnic humor, however, are not worth the effects that jokes may have on your total image. People may be offended.

Don't interrupt. People hate being interrupted. Fight the impulse to interrupt and give the person you're talking to the time they need to complete what they're saying to you.

Be enthusiastic and upbeat. Don't be afraid to show enthusiasm. It allows the other person to feel that you're interested in what they're saying to you.

Be flexible in your point of view. Try to be as open as possible, and try to see things from the other person's point of view.

There are also some signals that you can send to the other person that will bring the conversation to its close without hurting anyone's feelings. Breaking eye contact is a discreet signal that the conversation is about to end. Another way to signal is to use transition words like *well* or *at any rate*. You may want to recap all that was said. Whatever you do, don't lie to the other person. If you're not interested in talking to them again, don't mention the possibility of a future meeting, just to be polite. Instead, you may want to say, *"Nice meeting you."* And then, leave.

Finally, be sure to give the other person a good firm handshake. The final impression you make can be just as important as the initial one you made.

Topic discussion:

Work in pairs and exchange opinions with your partner on "How to be a good conversationalist?"

常用词汇和短语

商务联系和合作：

close relationship 密切的关系
conclude a business transaction 达成商务交易
continue business relationship 继续业务关系
cooperative relationship 合作关系
do business in a moderate way 稳重做生意
do business in a sincere way 诚恳做生意
enlarge/widen business relationship 扩大业务关系
improve business relationship 改善业务关系
interrupt business relationship 中断业务关系
maintain business relationship 保持业务关系
make a deal 做一笔交易
mutually beneficial relations 互利关系
promote business relationship 促进业务关系
reach an agreement 达成协议
reactivate business relationship 使业务

Unit 8 Building up Business Relations

关系重新活跃起来
restore/renew business relationship 恢复业务关系
scope of cooperation 合作范围
speed up business relationship 加快业务关系的发展
technological cooperation 技术合作
trade with 和……进行贸易

投资：

a heavy investment 一项巨额投资
a long-term investment 一项长期投资
a profitable investment 一项有利可图的投资
a safe and sure investment 一项安全可靠的投资
contractual joint venture 契约式合资企业
cooperative enterprise 合作企业
equity joint venture 股权式合资企业
exclusively foreign-owned enterprise 外商独资企业
foreign direct investment 国外直接投资
investment environment 投资环境
investment intent 投资意向
investment partner 投资伙伴
joint venture 合资企业
portfolio investment 间接投资，组合投资，证券投资

贸易形式：

assembling with supplied parts 来件装配
barter trade 易货贸易
bilateral trade 双边贸易
buy-back n. 回购
compensation trade 补偿贸易
consignment n. 寄售
counter purchase 互购贸易
counter trade 对销贸易
invisible trade 无形贸易
leasing trade 租赁贸易
merchandise exports and imports 货物进出口
processing with imported materials 进料加工
processing with supplied materials 来料加工
processing with supplied sample 来样加工
service exports and imports 服务进出口
visible trade 有形贸易

产品介绍：

attractive and durable　美观耐用
complete in specifications　规格齐全
durable consumer goods　耐用消费品
excellent quality　优良品质
genuine article　真货
high-tech products　高科技产品
imitation　n. 仿制品
inferior goods　劣质货
low-priced goods　廉价货
low-quality goods　次货
modern and elegant in fashion　式样新颖大方
reliable quality　质量可靠
showy goods　外观华丽的商品
skillful manufacture　制作精巧
sophisticated technology　工艺精良
superior quality　品质优异
top-grade goods　头等货
unfinished products　半成品
wide varieties　品种繁多

信用：

a sound business partner　很好的贸易伙伴
accord a credit　给予信赖
an objective opinion towards the company　对公司的客观评价
as a reference　作为资信人
business ability　经营能力
business scope/frame/range　经营范围
capital　n. 资金
capitalization　n. 资金状况
commercial credit　商业信用
competitive ability　竞争能力
competitive position　竞争地位
credit analysis　信用分析
credit appraisal　信用评价
credit enquiry　信用咨询
credit first　信用第一
credit insurance　信用保险
credit investigation　信用调查
credit position　信用状况
credit rating　信用等级
credit standing/status　资信状况
credit worthiness　资信，信誉
credit-worthy　a. 信用声誉好的
declare bankruptcy　宣告破产
enjoy a good reputation　享有好声誉
enjoy an unlimited credit　博得极大的信赖
financial ability　财务能力
financial position　财务状况
financial power　财力
financial standing　财务状态
form a picture of the company　对公司有粗略了解
guarantee the correctness　保证正确性
have a very high regard for　有很高的评价
hold sb. in the highest esteem　对某人

Unit 8 Building up Business Relations

推崇备至
indebtedness n. 负债状况
list of references 资信名册
modes of business 经营方式
registered capital 注册资本
reliability n. 可靠性

reliable reputation 信誉可靠
reputable a. 名声好的
safe firm 可靠的公司
satisfaction of customers 顾客的满意程度
trade reputation 贸易声誉

Unit

9

Application for Foreign Jobs

涉外工作申请

Learning Resources

Warming-up

1. Where and how to look for a job?

There are basically five ways to get a lead on a job: referral, respond to an advertisement, recruitment, cold calls to employers, and using an employment agency. All are valid and there is no reason why a candidate can't use all five methods at the same time.

Recruitment is one of the two best ways to find a job. The first is when you're at the top of your game and everybody in town wants you. That's the best possible way because you can basically write your own ticket. There really isn't an interview. You sort of skip that and go right into negotiations. In the business it is quietly referred to as stealing. It's when you recruit another company's people for your own staff.

The other type of recruiting, the one everybody agrees takes place at job fairs and on school campuses around graduation time. Large companies always need new people. They need the fresh ideas and new outlooks.

2. What to ask?

An applicant is free to ask any question he or she wants. The best ones are those that check on special requirements of this particular job. In other words, questions tell the interviewer that you want to do a good job. The following is an example of some good questions to ask: things that will tell the interviewer that if hired, you'll do your best to deliver the product.

Once again Mary is running the interview. Jack is the applicant asking some good questions, the kind that say: hire me and I'll give you your money's worth.

3. What to bring to the interview?

First, you have to bring yourself looking sharp. The only things you should have in there are a writing pad for making notes if you're old-fashioned, or a palm pilot if you're fully-automated. Bring two full sets of your paper work, letters of recommendation and a copy of the degrees you've earned, each in a separate envelope. You may be asked for another copy.

If during the interview, you notice the copy the interviewer has is marked up with notes, you can offer him or her a clean complete package. If the decision will be made by someone higher on the food chain, that means he or she is looking for the four or five finalists. When he or she selects them, he or she will

Unit 9 Application for Foreign Jobs

make up a report discussing every candidate and his or her perception of them. He or she will place his or her report on top and arrange the individual packages from each of the finalists in the order they'll be interviewed. He or she would love to have clean copies to make the packages for the executive that makes the decision.

If it's at all possible, you should bring examples of your work. If you have anything like that, they should work for you.

4. The job you're always wanted.

There is one last point you need to keep in mind if you want to have a successful career. You have to love your work. There are those who have to be challenged. Meeting new challenges makes them grow. It keeps them young and alive, sustaining them as they evolve spiritually and emotionally.

You can never go back. You have to move forward. Look for that new job. Grow and become the man or woman fated and the stars have made it possible for you to be. Good luck.

Dialogues

 **Dialogue 1** **Applying for a Job**

Li Na (L) wants to work for a big multinational company. She is calling the company on the telephone and talking with Mr. Bruce (B) who is in personnel department.

B: Good morning. May I help you?

L: Yes, my name is Li Na. I'd like to apply for a job with your company. Could you please tell me what procedure to follow?

B: Certainly. You could send us your resume in the mail with a cover letter, or you could bring it in yourself.

L: Thank you. Do you mind if I ask it you are interviewing now?

B: As a matter of fact, yes, we are. We have two positions available now. But you'd better hurry. We're planning to fill them within the three weeks, and we have a lot of applicants.

L: Thank you. Would it be all right if I come in this afternoon?

B: Yes, but we'll have to arrange an interview for some time later in this week.

L: That would be fine, thank you. Should I bring anything else with me?

B: No, but I'd like to ask you a question, if you don't mind.

L: Sure. What do you want to know?

B: How did you hear about our company? Did you see the ad in the newspaper?

L: No. Your company is very reputed in this city; I heard much praise to your company.

B: Oh, thank you. We'll see you this afternoon. You can ask for me when you come in.

L: Thank you. I'll be in at about 2:30.

B: That will be fine, Miss Li. Goodbye.

L: Goodbye.

Dialogue 2　Job Interview

Sally Fraser (S), a human resources officer for a medium-sized hotel on the West Coast, is interviewing Li Ming (L) for a position as a night manager.

S: Come in, Mr. Li. Please take a seat.

L: Thanks.

S: Mr. Li, did you graduate from Shanghai Foreign Language University?

L: Yes, I did.

S: Have you learned any other languages except English?

L: I have learned a little French.

S: Please tell me your strong points in one sentence.

L: I am a highly responsible and reliable person. If you give me the job, I shall try my best to do it.

S: I see from your resume that you certainly have the educational background and work background to handle this job. In fact, you seem to be somewhat overqualified for this job. It's not as high a position as head manager of a major hotel like you had on the East Coast. Why are you applying here?

L: From what I know, your hotel is very progressive and in a good position for expansion, and I think I can help you do that. I consider time management to be one of my key strengths. As a night manager, I think I can maximize my time to ensure

Unit 9 Application for Foreign Jobs

that night operations run at top efficiency, and at the same time help you plan your expansion.

S: I'm impressed with your advance knowledge of our business. Your cover letter shows that you've done your homework, and you have all the qualifications we're looking for. But I'm still a little worried that you'll leave if a higher position opens up at a more prominent hotel.

L: I came to the West Coast for a change of pace. The night position suits my goals for the present, and I'm looking forward to the challenge of helping to make your hotel one of the key players here.

S: I like your attitude, and it looks like you're the person for the job. The position's open two weeks from Monday. Can you start then?

L: No problem!

▶ Dialogue 3 About the Salary

Mr. Johnson (J), the manager in the export department, is discussing the treatment with Ms. Linda (L).

J: Good afternoon, Ms. Linda. Please sit down.

L: Thanks.

J: You live in Birmingham, don't you?

L: Yes.

J: How did you get here today, Linda?

L: I came here by coach this morning.

J: I hope you had a good journey.

L: Yes, thank you.

J: Well, now, let's see. We have received your recommendation and resume, and we thought we would like to ask you to come here for an interview.

L: It is a great pleasure for me to have this opportunity for interview.

J: Thank you for coming to our interview. Could you tell me why you applied for this job?

L: Frankly speaking, I am interested in being an interpreter. What's more, your company is a big multinational company. If I can work here, I'll have more opportunities to learn.

J: That's very good. You'd like to join our team, I gather.

L: Yes, I would.

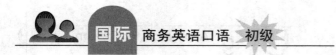

J: In this office, we encourage full attendance by offering a bonus. If you take any leaves or are late by over half an hour in a month, we'll deduct money from your salary.

L: I see. May I know the office hours?

J: Office hours are nine to six. One hour and thirty minutes for lunch.

L: How many days shall I work every week?

J: Five days.

L: I see.

J: Do you have any questions?

L: May I know how much I will be paid monthly?

J: We'll give you about four thousand yuan to start. There'll be a trial period of three months. One year later, we'll also have a job performance review and consider giving you a raise.

L: That's good. I think I like the job. How soon could I know the result?

J: We'll inform you in writing in a week if you are accepted.

L: Thank you. I'll be looking forward to hearing from you.

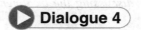 **Dialogue 4 Telling the Result of Interview**

Mr. Peter (P), the manager in the export department, is calling Yang Le (Y) on the telephone and telling her the result of interview.

P: Good morning. This is ABC Corporation. May I speak to Yang Le?

Y: This is Yang Le speaking.

P: I'm calling to offer you the position of account.

Y: I really appreciate the offer.

P: Please come to work this Thursday.

Y: Great, thank you very much. You know I'm desiring to work in your company,

P: What's your expected salary?

Y: What is important to me is the job and the people I will be working with, so regarding salary, I leave it to you and I am sure that you will make me a fair offer.

P: I can offer you 5,000 yuan per month. Raises are given after probation period according to your performance. Is this satisfactory?

Y: Yes, it is quite satisfactory. I accept it.

P: Any other questions?

Unit 9 Application for Foreign Jobs

Y: Yes, how long is the probation period?
P: One month.
Y: I see. Thanks.

Words and Expressions

multinational company 多国公司	maximize v. 使增加至最大限度，求……的最大值
resume n. 简历	at top efficiency 高效
applicant n. 申请人	prominent a. 卓越的，重要的，著名的
human resources 人力资源	bonus n. 奖金，补贴
night manager 夜班经理	probation period 试用期，见习期

求 职 面 试

　　作为一名中国人，在申请涉外工作时，你会发现国籍所带来的好处和坏处。在你走进求职公司的大门，或和对方以电话安排会谈之前，人事主管早已对你有了一定的看法。这些看法的正确与否，要根据他之前和中国人打交道的经历来判断。如果你是他认识的第一个中国人，那么他对你的看法则是中国人给许多美国人留下的刻板印象。例如，并非所有美国新移民都有很好的名声，但一般来说，亚洲人的信誉都很好，特别是中国人，其中尤以那些从事高科技产业的人的名声最佳。中国人以诚实、认真工作闻名，同时也很忠诚、友善，力求将工作做好，但有时因为语言和口音问题，使彼此的沟通并不容易。雇用非英语系国家的人，唯一可能的缺点就是口语沟通能力较差，但任何种族的人都可能有这种问题。因此建议大家要尽量练习说英语、听英语，重要的是，要记住面试时让你可以表现英语听、说技巧的机会，要善用这个机会。

　　面试对于求职者来说至关重要。就公司而言，受试者的教育程度及经验固然重要，然而求职者的心理状态也不容忽视，这也正是面试方在面试中所极为关心的。

　　在面试时，作为一个受试者，你的外表是你给人的第一印象，所以你的外表应尽可能令人愉快，着装职业化，当然最重要的是整洁大方，恰如其分。良好的仪表无疑也会让你在面试中显得更为自信。其实，受试者在张口说话之前，就已经受到了审视，面试者已经对你的个性、判断力以及灵活性等方面加以评价了。当然你的才能还会通过你的言谈表现出来，那么怎样才能更好地表现你自己呢？

面试前要尽量多了解公司的情况，若能找到公司简介，要认真阅读公司有关的产品介绍、政策和发展潜力等内容。你对公司的兴趣和主动性会给面试者留下深刻印象。

面试时，通常碰到的话题为以往的工作、所受的教育与培训、专业与课程、业余爱好、外语程度、个人能力和福利待遇等方面的内容。为了在面试过程中避免说出不适当的话，请注意以下几点，并熟悉和掌握常用的句型和表达。

（1）面试前就对所申请工作的职责和起薪有充分的了解，谈谈你自己在这方面的兴趣和经验。

（2）要谈出自己接受过的教育、培训和资历。训练一下如何表述自己的家庭、学历、爱好等内容。

（3）如有工作经验，要准备扼要地描述以前的工作情况。不要批评前一任雇主。

（4）等面试者提出薪金的问题时，才说明你所期望的待遇。

（5）面试者在对你提问完毕后总会问："好，你有什么问题吗？"你可以询问公司的发展计划以及产品方面的问题，不过下面的问题应避免：

* What, exactly, does your company do? 不要问这种在公司简介中查一下就能得到答案的问题。

* What does the job pay? 在面试者向你提问之前，避免讨论薪酬的问题。

* How many vacations and personal days do you allow? 这样的问题使你显得懒惰。

* How long will it take me to get promotion? 太直接，你可用较委婉的提法：Can you describe what my career-advancement track might be like?

* Is that your wife in the picture on your desk? 不要谈论个人问题。

* What are you going to do about the poor performance of product X? 应正面提问：What plan do you have to build sales for product X?

* What's your company's track record on promoting women and minorities? 这是个合理的问题，但面试者可能担心你如果晋升不快会起诉他们。还是通过本行业内线来了解公司的声誉为好。

* So, when do I start? 问得好，但有点儿让人讨厌。好像让人觉得不请自来。

1. What kind of vacancies do you have?
   你们有哪些职位空缺？

Unit 9　Application for Foreign Jobs

2. Is this vacancy still available?
   这个职位还招人吗?

3. What are the requirements to apply for the position?
   应聘这个职位的条件是什么?

4. I'm inquiring about the job.
   我想询问一下有关这份工作的情况。

5. What should I do to apply for the position?
   我应该怎样应聘这个职位?

6. When is Mr. Li available?
   李先生什么时候有时间?

7. I wonder whether you have received my resume.
   我想知道你们是否收到了我的简历。

8. Here is my recommendation.
   这是我的推荐信。

9. Are these all your credentials?
   这些都是你的证明材料吗?

10. Which position would you recommend?
    你推荐哪一个职位?

11. You'll need to give me a copy of your resume first.
    先给我一份你的个人简历吧。

12. Do you require an English resume?
    你们要求提供英文简历吗?

13. How about your present pay?
    你现在的薪水是多少?

14. I'd like to start at about 1,500 yuan a month.
    我希望底薪为每月 1 500 元左右。

15. How about vacations?
    休假情况是怎样的?

16. Besides you may have a paid month holiday every year.
    此外你每年可休一个月的带薪假。

17. You'll get bonuses at the end of each year.
    每年你都会得到年终奖金。

18. We do expect you to work overtime when it is necessary.
    必要时我们需要你能加班。

Exercises

I Complete the following dialogues.

1. **A:** How did you hear about this position?
   B: _____.
   （我从网上得知的。）
2. **A:** Do you know something about our company?
   B: Yes. This is a great company. _____.
   （而且贵公司的产品很畅销。）I know you could use someone like me.
3. **A:** We have received your recommendation and resume, and we thought we would like to ask you to come here for an interview.
   B: _____.
   （我非常高兴有这个面试机会。）
4. **A:** What makes you think you would be a success in this position?
   B: _____.
   （我在学校所学的知识和我的工作经验会使我胜任这份工作。）I am sure I will be successful.
5. **A:** Do you give a bonus?
   B: Yes, we do. _____.
   （如果生意好，每月的奖金会很丰厚。）
6. **A:** I think I like the job. How soon could I know the result?
   B: _____.
   （如果你被录用，我们将在一周内书面通知你。）
7. **A:** I can offer you 5,000 yuan per month. _____
   _____?
   （试用期后将根据工作表现加薪，你满意吗？）
   B: Yes, it is quite satisfactory. I accept it.

II Situational practice.

1. **The situation:** You have seen an advertisement in a local newspaper about the recruitment of a secretary.
   The task: Phone the personnel office of ABC Company to let them know you are interested in the post and tell them briefly about yourself.
2. **The situation:** You are a college graduate majoring in international trade. You are now

Unit 9 Application for Foreign Jobs

looking for a job. CSB Company, a large and well-known international trading company, is recruiting new staff.

The task: You apply for a job with the company and are asked to be interviewed by the personnel manager.

对话汉译

对话 1 申请职位

李娜（L）想进一家大的跨国公司工作，她正在电话里与这家公司人事部的布鲁斯先生（B）交谈。

B: 早上好。您有什么事吗？
L: 是的，我叫李娜。我想参加贵公司的应聘。您能告诉我手续怎么办吗？
B: 好的。你需要给我发一封带有求职信和个人简历的邮件，或者亲自送过来也行。
L: 谢谢。请问你们正在面试吗？
B: 是的，我们正在进行面试。我们现在有两个职位空缺。但是你得抓紧时间。我们打算在三周内把职位补全。目前有很多应聘人员。
L: 谢谢。请问我今天下午可以到公司来一趟吗？
B: 好的，但是得在这周晚些时候安排面试。
L: 好的，非常感谢。我还需要带其他东西吗？
B: 不用，如果你不介意的话，我有个问题想要问你。
L: 当然。您想问什么？
B: 你是如何了解到我们公司的相关信息的？从报纸上的广告看到的吗？
L: 不是，贵公司在本市很有名，我听到过很多对贵公司的好评。
B: 谢谢，下午见。下午来公司的时候可以直接找我。
L: 谢谢。我下午2点半来公司。
B: 好的，李小姐。再见。
L: 再见。

对话 2 工作面试

来自西海岸一家中型酒店人力资源部的萨利·弗瑞泽(S)正在就夜班经理一职对李明(L)

125

进行面试。

S: 请进，李先生请坐。
L: 谢谢。
S: 李先生是上海外国语大学毕业的吗？
L: 是的。
S: 除了英语，还会哪国外语？
L: 会一点儿法语。
S: 请用一句话说一下您的优点。
L: 责任感强、可靠是我的优点。如果能给我在这儿工作的机会的话，我保证尽全力努力工作。
S: 我从您的简历中看出，您有足够的教育背景和工作背景来接手这份工作。事实上，您的能力有点太突出了。我们这里的职位不像您在东海岸的大型酒店工作时所担任的总经理那样高。您为什么要应聘到这里工作呢？
L: 据我所知，你们的酒店发展很快，业务扩展进程也进行得很顺利，我想我在这方面可以助你们一臂之力。我认为时间管理是我的强项之一。作为夜班经理，我想我能最大限度地利用我的时间来保证酒店夜间服务工作以最高效率运行，同时我还能帮助你们扩展业务。
S: 您对我们业务情况的预先了解给我留下了深刻的印象。您的求职信表明您做了预先的准备工作并且具备我们需要的一切资质条件。但我还是有点担心，如果另一家更优秀的酒店向您提供更高的职位，您就会离开了。
L: 我来西海岸是为了改变我的生活节奏。这份夜间工作正切合我目前的目标，我期待着迎接挑战来帮助你们成为本地最重要的酒店之一。
S: 我欣赏您的态度，看起来您是这份工作最合适的人选了。这个职位在下周一后的两个星期就空下来了。您到时候能开始工作吗？
L: 没问题。

▶ 对话 3　关于薪酬问题

约翰逊先生（J）是公司出口部的经理，他正在和琳达女士（L）讨论待遇问题。

J: 下午好，琳达女士。请坐。
L: 谢谢。
J: 你住在伯明翰，是吗？
L: 是的。
J: 今天你是怎么到这儿的？

Unit 9　Application for Foreign Jobs

L: 我早上坐长途汽车过来的。
J: 希望你这次旅途愉快！
L: 是的，谢谢。
J: 嗯，现在我们步入正题。我们收到了你的推荐信和个人简历，我们希望你来参加面试。
L: 我非常高兴有这个面试机会。
J: 感谢你来参加我们的应聘。你能告诉我应聘的理由吗？
L: 坦白说，我对口译的工作很感兴趣。而且，贵公司是大型跨国公司，如果我能在这儿工作的话，对我来说会有更多的学习机会。
J: 很好。我猜测你也想加入我们公司吧。
L: 是的，我想加入。
J: 我们公司提供全勤奖来鼓励员工全勤。如果一个月内请假或是迟到半小时的话，我们就会扣薪水。
L: 我了解。请问上班时间是几点呢？
J: 早上九点到下午六点。中午有一个半小时的用餐时间。
L: 每周工作几天？
J: 五天。
L: 我明白了。
J: 你还有其他的问题吗？
L: 请问我每个月的薪水是多少呢？
J: 底薪四千元左右。还有三个月的试用期。一年以后，我们会有一个工作表现评价会，再考虑要不要给你加薪。
L: 那很好。我想我喜欢这份工作。贵公司多快能让我知道结果？
J: 如果录用你的话，一周后会发书面通知给你。
L: 谢谢。期待贵公司的消息。

▶ 对话4　通知面试结果

彼得先生（P）是公司出口部的经理，他正在电话中通知杨乐（Y）面试的结果。

P: 早上好，这里是 ABC 公司。请问杨乐在吗？
Y: 我就是。
P: 我们决定聘用你为会计。
Y: 很感激贵公司的录用。
P: 请于周四来上班。
Y: 好的，非常感谢。您知道我渴望能为贵公司工作。

P: 你期望的薪资是多少？

Y: 对我来说，工作及同事较为重要，至于薪资，留给您来决定，我相信您会给我一个合理的薪资的。

P: 我可以给你一个月 5 000 元。试用期后将根据工作表现加薪，你满意吗？

Y: 是的，我很满意，我可以接受这一安排。

P: 还有什么问题吗？

Y: 有，请问试用期多长时间？

P: 一个月。

Y: 我知道了，谢谢。

Extended Reading

Marcela's Work Experience

I decided early in my college years that I wanted to experience living abroad before entering in the "real world". During my senior year, while most of my friends were interviewing for "real world" jobs, I was investigating how I could go work in a different country. At that early stage of my inquiry I was pretty open about where to go and what kind of work to undertake. My desire to live abroad was so strong that I was willing to do anything anywhere.

Soon I learned about BUNAC, a program that seemed to be designed precisely for students with such interests. BUNAC offers work visas for students or recent graduates to work overseas. Of the six countries available, I chose England because of the language and opportunities for employment.

Two months after I graduated from college I crossed the Atlantic. I traveled throughout Europe for six weeks before arriving in London. I got to London on August 24, 1997 with a work visa, but no job or place to live. I have to admit it was pretty scary! The day after I arrived, I experienced my first British holiday—a Bank Holiday, a national holiday where everything is closed for the day. It wasn't until my third day that I visited the BUNAC office and went through orientation. At the orientation I learned all about living and working in Britain; I learned about getting around in the city, making a CV (Curriculum Vitae—British resume), paying taxes, getting health insurance, traveling around Britain, finding accommodations and most importantly, finding a job. I was most scared about finding a job since my financial resources were running low and I needed to get a paycheck soon.

It turns out that finding a job was just as easy as making a CV! The BUNAC program is

Unit 9 Application for Foreign Jobs

very well known in London and many employers participate in the program. As a result there are many employers in many different fields to choose from. My job search began when I chose three different business employers and faxed them my cover letter and CV. That first week I had three interviews. I accepted my first offer working for Merrill Lynch International Bank. The Merrill Lynch office I worked at was in a beautiful, old building located two blocks from Buckingham Palace. The people were nice and the work interesting.

It was easy to adjust to life in London. And there is so much to see that after six months exploring I probably covered only half of what I intended.

Working in London has many advantages. For one, I truly get to learn the culture by being immersed in its workforce. Most of my coworkers were British so I feel like I really got to know and learn the British culture through such a huge aspect of a British person's daily life. Secondly, it is an economical way to live and travel in another country since most jobs pay enough to cover rent, living expenses and some travel expenses. And thirdly, I have the chance to gain valuable work experience and internationalize my resume.

Working in London has been the best decision I have made so far. I would not hesitate for a second to recommend it to anyone!

Topic discussion:

Do you have any working experience? What kind of work do you think you would enjoy?

常用词汇和短语

个人资料:
birth date   出生日期
birthplace   n. 出生地点
country   n. 国家, 故乡
current/present address   现住址
family status   家庭状况
far-sighted   a. 远视的, 有远见的
marital status   婚姻状况
married   a. 已婚的

native place   籍贯
permanent address   永久住址
prefecture   n. 辖区
province   n. 省
short-sighted   a. 近视的, 目光短浅的
single/unmarried   a. 未婚的, 单身的
town   n. 城镇

国际商务英语口语 初级

教育背景：

bachelor n. 学士	minor v. 辅修
certificate n. 资格证书	part-time job 兼职工作
courses taken/completed 所学课程	post doctorate 博士后
curriculum included 所含课程	refresher course 进修课程
doctor n. 博士	reward n. 奖励
extracurricular activities 课外活动	scholarship n. 奖学金
major v. 主修	social activity 社会活动
master n. 硕士	social practice 社会实践

个人性格：

adaptable a. 适应性强的，能适应的	independent a. 有主见的
ambitious a. 有雄心的	introverted a. 内向的
analytical a. 善于分析的	motivated a. 目标明确的
aspiring a. 有抱负的	objective a. 客观的
capable a. 能干的	open-minded a. 虚心的
contemplative a. 好沉思的	outgoing a. 外向的
cooperative a. 有合作精神的	persevering a. 不屈不挠的
creative a. 创新的	practical a. 实际的
dedicated a. 有奉献精神的	punctual a. 守时的
dynamic a. 有活力的	purposeful a. 意志坚强的，有决心的
easy-going a. 随和的	realistic a. 实事求是的
efficient a. 效率高的	reliable a. 可信赖的
energetic a. 精力充沛的	responsible a. 有责任心的
enthusiastic a. 热情的	self-conscious a. 自觉的
extroverted a. 外向的	straightforward a. 老实的
hardworking/industrious/diligent a. 勤奋的	strong-willed a. 意志坚强的
	tireless a. 孜孜不倦的
honest a. 诚实的	well-educated a. 受过良好教育的
hospitable a. 好客的	well-trained a. 受过良好训练的
humorous a. 幽默的	

Unit 9 Application for Foreign Jobs

工作经验：

accomplish　*v.*　完成（任务）
appointed　*a.*　被任命的
authorized　*a.*　被委任的
design　*v.*　设计
develop　*v.*　开发
direct　*v.*　指导
enliven　*v.*　使活跃，使有生气
enrich　*v.*　使丰富
exploit　*v.*　开发（资源）
initiate　*v.*　开创
innovate　*v.*　改革，创新
integrate　*v.*　使结合
introduce　*v.*　引进
invent　*v.*　发明
motivate　*v.*　促进
nominated　*a.*　被提名的
organize　*v.*　组织
originate　*v.*　创始
participate in　参加

perform　*v.*　履行
promote　*v.*　推销，提升，促进
promoted to　被提升为
proposed as　被提名为
recommended　*a.*　被推荐的
reconsolidate　*v.*　重新巩固
regenerate　*v.*　更新
regularize　*v.*　使系统化
reinforce　*v.*　加强
renovate　*v.*　革新
replace　*v.*　接替
resolve　*v.*　解决
shorten　*v.*　缩短，减少
simplify　*v.*　简化
sponsor　*v.*　主办
supervise　*v.*　监督
systematize　*v.*　使系统化
verify　*v.*　证实
vivify　*v.*　使活跃

其他：

a challenging opportunity　有挑战的机会
achievement　*n.*　工作业绩
benefits　*n.*　福利待遇
career objective　职业目标
job objective　工作目标
opportunities for further education　深造的机会
opportunities for personal development　个人发展的机会

position applied for　申请的职位
position desired　期望的职位
position　*n.*　职位
promotion　*n.*　晋升
prospects of promotion　晋升机会
recommendation　*n.*　推荐
reference letter　推荐信
responsibility　*n.*　职责
salary　*n.*　薪水，工资
wage　*n.*　工资，报酬

Appendix A Glossary
词 汇 表

Words
单　词

accessory　*n*.　零件，配件
accompany　*v*.　伴随，陪伴
accomplish　*v*.　完成（任务）
accountant　*n*.　会计
achievement　*n*.　工作业绩
adaptable　*a*.　适应性强的，能适应的
administrative　*a*.　行政的，管理的
agreement　*n*.　协议，协定
air-conditioned　*a*.　有空调的
ambitious　*a*.　有雄心的
analytical　*a*.　善于分析的
anniversary　*n*.　周年纪念
annual　*a*.　每年的，年度的
applicant　*n*.　申请人
applicant　*n*.　申请人
appoint　*v*.　任命，约定（时间、地点等）
appointed　*a*.　被任命的
appointment　*n*.　约定，约会
appreciate　*v*.　感激
armchair　*n*.　扶手椅
article　*n*.　物件
ashtray　*n*.　烟灰缸
aspiring　*a*.　有抱负的
assistant　*n*.　助理

attempt　*n*.　尝试，努力
attendant　*n*.　服务员
auditor　*n*.　查账员，审计员
authorized　*a*.　被委任的
automated　*a*.　机械化的，自动的
available　*a*.　可找到的，空闲的，可利用的，可获得的
bachelor　*n*.　学士
background　*n*.　背景
baggage　*n*.　行李
balcony　*n*.　阳台
banker　*n*.　银行家
bar　*n*.　酒吧间
barber　*n*.　为男士理发的理发师
basement　*n*.　地下室
bathrobe　*n*.　浴衣
bathroom　*n*.　浴室
bedroom　*n*.　卧铺
bedspread　*n*.　床罩
bench　*n*.　板凳
beneficial　*a*.　有益的
benefits　*n*.　福利待遇
bill　*n*.　账单
birthplace　*n*.　出生地点

Appendix A Glossary

blur v. 使……模糊不清
bonus n. 奖金，补贴
book v. 预订
booking n. 预订
boost v. 提高
bother v. 麻烦，打扰
brand n. 牌子，商标
brochure n. 小册子
broker n. 经纪人
bulb n. 灯泡
businessman n. 商人
buy-back n. 回购
call v. 打电话
campaign n. 战役，运动
cancellation n. 取消
candidate n. 求职者，候选人
canteen n. 食堂，小卖部
canvass v. 征求意见，劝说
capable a. 能干的
capacity n. 生产量，生产力
capital n. 资金
capitalization n. 资金状况
cellar n. 地窖
certificate n. 资格证书
client n. 委托人，顾客
clinic n. 门诊所
cloakroom n. 寄存处
clothes-hanger n. 衣架
committee n. 委员会
concerned a. 有关的
confirm v. 确定，确认
confiscate v. 没收，征用
consignment n. 寄售
consultant n. 咨询员，顾问
container n. 容器，集装箱

contemplative a. 好沉思的
contraband n. 违禁品，走私
contract n. 合同，契约
contractor n. 承办商，承建人
cooperative a. 有合作精神的
country n. 国家，故乡
creative a. 创新的
credit-worthy a. 信用声誉好的
curtain n. 窗帘
cushion n. 垫子
declaration n. （纳税品）申报，报告，报关
declare v. 宣告，声明，报关
dedicated a. 有奉献精神的
delay v. 推迟
deluxe n. 豪华的
departure n. 离开
deposit n. 储蓄，保证金，订金
design v. 设计
destination n. 目的地
develop v. 开发
diner n. 餐车
direct v. 指导
discount n. 折扣
dispatch v. 调遣
display v. 展出，显示
dispose v. 安排，处理（事务）
distribution n. 分配，分发，分送产品
divisions/departments n. 部门
doctor n. 博士
draft n. 草稿
drawback n. 退税
duty n. 税
duty-free a. 免税的
dynamic a. 有活力的

133

easy-going *a.* 随和的
edge *n.* 优势，优越之处
efficient *a.* 效率高的
energetic *a.* 精力充沛的
enliven *v.* 使活跃，使有生气
enquiry *n.* 询问
enrich *v.* 使丰富
enthusiastic *a.* 热情的
evaluation *n.* 评估
exempt *v.* 免税，免除
exhibit *n.* 陈列品
expenditure *n.* 花费，支出额
expense *n.* 费用，支出
expertise *n.* 专业知识
exploit *v.* 开发（资源）
extension *n.* 延长（日期），（电话）分机
extroverted *a.* 外向的
facility *n.* 设备
far-sighted *a.* 远视的，有远见的
fetch *v.* 接来，取来
fine *n.&v.* 罚款
follow *v.* 听懂，领会
foodstuff *n.* 粮食，食品
forward *v.* 发送，寄发
free *a.* 有空的
gross *a.* 总的，毛的，总共的
group *n.* 集团
guarantee *v.* 保证
hairdresser *n.* 理发师，美容师，美发厅，美容厅
handle *v.* 处理，操作
hardworking/industrious/diligent *a.* 勤奋的
headquarters *n.* 总部

helmet *n.* 安全帽，头盔
honest *a.* 诚实的
hospitable *a.* 好客的
humorous *a.* 幽默的
imitation *n.* 仿制品
impressive *a.* 给人印象深刻的
indebtedness *n.* 负债状况
independent *a.* 有主见的
ingredient *n.* 成分，因素
initiate *v.* 开创
innovate *v.* 改革，创新
inspect *v.* 检查
inspection *n.* 检验
integrate *v.* 使结合
introduce *v.* 引进
introverted *a.* 内向的
invent *v.* 发明
itinerary *n.* 旅游计划，日程安排
lag *v.* 走得慢，落后
lampshade *n.* 灯罩
layover *n.* 中途停留
list *n.* 名单，列表
literature *n.* 商品说明书之类的印刷宣传品
lobby *n.* 大厅，休息室
lounge *n.* 酒店大堂
lucrative *a.* 获利的
major *v.* 主修
manager *n.* 经理
managerial *a.* 管理的
manufacture *n.* 制造业
married *a.* 已婚的
master *n.* 硕士
mat *n.* 席
mattress *n.* 褥子

Appendix A　Glossary

maximize　v.　使增加至最大限度，求……的最大值
merge　v.　（企业、团体等）合并
minor　v.　辅修
minute　n.　记录，会议纪要
mirror　n.　镜子
monthly　a.　每月的
motivate　v.　促进
motivated　a.　目标明确的
mushroom　n.　蘑菇
nationality　n.　国籍
negotiation　n.　谈判，磋商
newsstand　n.　售报处
nightstand　n.　床头柜
nominated　a.　被提名的
non-stop　a.　中间不停靠任何地方的
objective　a.　客观的
open-minded　a.　虚心的
operator　n.　电话接线员
organize　v.　组织
originate　v.　创始
outgoing　a.　外向的
output　n.　产量
output　n.　产量，出产
overtime　n.　加班时间，延长时间
passport　n.　护照
pay (=wage/salary)　n.　工资
payday　n.　发工资日，付薪日
payroll　n.　薪水册，工资单
peg/hook　n.　衣钩
perform　v.　履行
performance　n.　（机器等）工作性能
persevering　a.　不屈不挠的
pesticide　n.　农药
pillow　n.　枕头
pillowcase　n.　枕套
pilot　n.　驾驶员
plot　n.　剧情
plug　n.　插头
position　n.　职位
practical　a.　实际的
prefecture　n.　辖区
preference　n.　特惠，优先
presentation　n.　陈述
press　n.　报业，新闻界
profile　n.　简介
programmer　n.　电脑程序员
prominent　a.　卓越的，重要的，著名的
promote　v.　推销，提升，促进
promotion　n.　晋升
prop　n.　道具
proposal　n.　提议
province　n.　省
publisher　n.　出版人员，出版商
punctual　a.　守时的
purchaser　n.　采购员
purposeful　a.　意志坚强的，有决心的
qualification　n.　资格
quilt　n.　棉被
quote　v.　开（价）
radiator　n.　暖气片
reach　v.　找到
realistic　a.　实事求是的
receptionist　n.　接待员
recommend　v.　推荐
recommendation　n.　推荐
recommended　a.　被推荐的
reconfirm　v.　再次确定，再次确认
reconnect　v.　使重新接通
reconsolidate　v.　重新巩固

redundancy n. 过剩，多余，累赘
redundant a. 过剩的，多余的
regenerate v. 更新
registration n. 登记
regularize v. 使系统化
regulation n. 规章，规定，条例
reinforce v. 加强
reliability n. 可靠性
reliable a. 可信赖的
remuneration n. 报酬
renovate v. 革新
replace v. 接替
reputable a. 名声好的
reservation n. 保留，（宾馆房间等）预订
reservation n. 预订
reserve v. 预订
residue n. 残余，剩余，渣滓
resolve v. 解决
responsibility n. 职责
responsible a. 有责任心的
resume n. 简历
retailer n. 零售商
reward n. 奖励
rock-bottom a. 最低的，最低水平的，最低限度的
rug n. 小地毯
salary n. 薪水，工资
salesman n. 销售员
saleswoman n. 女店员
sampling n. 抽样，取样
scan v. 扫描
scene n. 情景
scholarship n. 奖学金
screen n. 屏，幕，屏风
secretary n. 秘书
section n. 部门，处，科，组
security n. 安全
self-conscious a. 自觉的
sheet n. 床单
shift n. 轮班
shop n. 小卖部
shopkeeper n. 店主
shorten v. 缩短，减少
short-sighted a. 近视的，目光短浅的
shuffle v. 推开，推诿
shutters n. 百叶窗
sightseeing n. 观光
sign v. 签单
signature n. 签名
simplify v. 简化
single/unmarried a. 未婚的，单身的
slipper n. 拖鞋
socket n. 插座
sponge n. 海绵
sponsor v. 主办
sprinkle-nozzle/(shower) nozzle n. 喷头
stenographer n. 速记员
stool n. 凳子
straightforward a. 老实的
strong-willed a. 意志坚强的
suitcase n. 手提箱，衣箱
suite n. 套房
supervise v. 监督
supervisor n. 主管人
switch n. 开关
systematize v. 使系统化
tariff n. 税则，关税
textile n. 纺织品
thermometer n. 温度计

词汇表 Appendix A Glossary

thoughtfulness n. 思虑，慎重
tireless a. 孜孜不倦的
toilet/lavatory/washroom n. 卫生间
towel n. 毛巾
town n. 城镇
tracer n. 绘图员
trademark n. 商标
transom (=transom window) n. 气窗
vacancy n. （职位）空缺
valid a. 有效的
variety n. 品种
verify v. 证实
vivify v. 使活跃
wage n. 工资，报酬
waiter n. （餐厅）服务员
waitress n. （餐厅）女服务员
wardrobe n. 衣柜
warehouse n. 仓库
washbasin n. 洗脸盆
well-educated a. 受过良好教育的
well-trained a. 受过良好训练的
wholesaler n. 批发商
windowsill n. 窗台
workforce n. 劳动力

Expressions
短　　语

a challenging opportunity 有挑战的机会
a heavy investment 一项巨额投资
a long-term investment 一项长期投资
a profitable investment 一项有利可图的投资
a safe and sure investment 一项安全可靠的投资
a sound business partner 很好的贸易伙伴
ABN AMRO 荷兰银行
accord a credit 给予信赖
accounts department 会计部，财务部
administration department 行政管理部
administrative staff 行政人员
advertising agency 广告代理商
advertising department 广告部
advertising effect 广告效应
air hostess 女乘务员，空姐
an objective opinion towards the company 对公司的客观评价
apply for 申请
as a reference 作为资信人
assembling with supplied parts 来件装配
assembly line 装配线
assembly plant 装配工厂
at top efficiency 高效
attractive and durable 美观耐用
bad quality 劣质
barter trade 易货贸易
basic wage 基础工资
bath towel 浴巾
bath tub 浴缸
bayonet-type bulb 卡口灯泡
bedside lamp 床头灯
bilateral trade 双边贸易
billiard room 台球房
birth date 出生日期

137

book keeper　记账员
broom closet　杂物室
built-in wardrobe (=closet)　壁橱
bulb holder　灯头
business ability　经营能力
business card　名片
business class　商务舱
business scope　经营范围
business scope/frame/range　经营范围
call on　呼吁，约请，拜访
cancel an appointment　取消约会
career objective　职业目标
cell phone　手机
central heating　中央暖气
change an appointment　更改约会
close relationship　密切的关系
club car　设有娱乐室的车厢
coincide with　与……相符
cold and hot water tap　冷热自来水龙头
commercial credit　商业信用
compensation trade　补偿贸易
competitive ability　竞争能力
competitive position　竞争地位
complete in specifications　规格齐全
conclude a business transaction　达成商务交易
confirm an appointment　确定约会
continue business relationship　继续业务关系
contractual joint venture　契约式合资企业
cooperative enterprise　合作企业
cooperative relationship　合作关系
cotton terry blanket　毛巾被
counter purchase　互购贸易
counter sample　对等样品

counter trade　对销贸易
courses taken/completed　所学课程
credit analysis　信用分析
credit appraisal　信用评价
credit enquiry　信用咨询
credit first　信用第一
credit insurance　信用保险
credit investigation　信用调查
credit position　信用状况
credit rating　信用等级
credit standing/status　资信状况
credit worthiness　资信，信誉
current/present address　现住址
curriculum included　所含课程
curriculum vitae (CV)　简历，履历
customer account department　客户账务部
customs broker　报关行
customs documents　海关文件，海关单据
customs duty (=tariff)　关税
customs invoice　海关发票
cut off　（指电话）通话被中断
daily wage　日工资
deal with　处理
declaration for export (=export declaration)
　出口申报单
declaration for import (=import declaration)
　进口申报单
declare bankruptcy　宣告破产
delivery order　提货单
desk clerk　值班服务员
desk lamp　台灯
differential duties　差别关税
dining room/dining hall　餐厅
dispose of　去掉，清除
distribution department　分销部

Appendix A Glossary

do business in a moderate way 稳重做生意
do business in a sincere way 诚恳做生意
Doing what we gotta do. 别无他法
door mat 门前的擦鞋棕垫
double bed 双人床
double room 双人房
draw up 草拟
dressing table 梳妆台
drop in 顺便去，顺道去
durable consumer goods 耐用消费品
dutiable goods 应纳税的货物
easy chair 安乐椅
economy class 经济舱
electric fan 电扇
electric iron 电熨斗
enjoy a good reputation 享有好声誉
enjoy an unlimited credit 博得极大的信赖
enlarge/widen business relationship 扩大业务关系
entrance fee 入港手续费
equity joint venture 股权式合资企业
evasion of duty 逃税
excellent quality 优良品质
excise duty 国内消费税
excitation mechanism 激励机制
exclusively foreign-owned enterprise 外商独资企业
expense account 费用账户
extra pay (=premium/bonus) 奖励，奖金
extracurricular activities 课外活动
family status 家庭状况
financial ability 财务能力
financial director 财务总监
financial position 财务状况
financial power 财力
financial services department 财务服务部
financial standing 财务状态
first class 头等舱
first-class quality 头等质量，头等品质
flight duration 飞行时间
flight schedule 飞机时刻表
floor lamp 落地灯
fluorescent lamp 日光灯
folding chair 折叠椅
foreign direct investment 国外直接投资
form a picture of the company 对公司有粗略了解
forwarding address 转投地址，转寄地址
forwarding company 运输公司
free goods 免税品
front desk 服务台
frosted bulb 磨砂灯泡
full-time employment/full-time job/full-time work 全职工作
genuine article 真货
go sightseeing 观光
graphic designer 美术设计员，平面设计师
gross wage 全部工资
guarantee the correctness 保证正确性
hang up/hang on 挂断电话/不挂断电话
hat rack 帽架
have a very high regard for 有很高的评价
have an appointment with sb. 与某人有个约会
head office 总部
high quality 高质量
high-tech products 高科技产品
hold sb. in the highest esteem 对某人推崇备至
hold the line （打电话时）不挂断

139

hourly wage/wage rate per hour 计时工资
human resources department 人力资源部
human resources 人力资源
import tariff 进口关税
improve business relationship 改善业务关系
inferior goods 劣质货
information desk 问询台
international practice 国际惯例
interrupt business relationship 中断业务关系
introductions and the agenda 介绍和会议议程
investment environment 投资环境
investment intent 投资意向
investment partner 投资伙伴
invisible trade 无形贸易
item on the agenda 议程项目
job objective 工作目标
joint venture 合资企业
keep an appointment 如期赴约
key puncher 电脑操作员
lace curtain 挑花窗帘，蕾丝窗帘
ladies' room 女盥洗室
laundry service 洗衣服务
leasing trade 租赁贸易
list of references 资信名册
local public service employee 地方公务员
long-term business relations 长期的业务关系
low-priced goods 廉价货
low-quality goods 次货
maintain business relationship 保持业务关系
maintenance department 维修部

major markets 主要市场
make a deal 做一笔交易
make an appointment 约会，预约
management department 管理部
marital status 婚姻状况
market potential 市场潜力
marketing department 营销部
maximum wage (=wage ceiling) 最高工资
men's room 男盥洗室
merchandise exports and imports 货物进出口
minimum wage 最低工资
modern and elegant in fashion 式样新颖大方
modes of business 经营方式
monthly wage 月工资
most favored nation clause 最惠国条款
multinational company 多国公司
mutually beneficial relations 互利关系
national tariff 国定税率，自主关税
native place 籍贯
net/real wage 实际收入，净收入
night manager 夜班经理
office girl 女记事员
one-way ticket 单程机票
opal bulb/opaque bulb 乳白灯泡
opportunities for further education 深造的机会
opportunities for personal development 个人发展的机会
packaging department 包装部
participate in 参加
part-time employment/part-time job/ part-time work 兼职工作
part-time job 兼职工作

Appendix A Glossary

pay slip　工资单
payment in kind　用实物付酬
pendant lamp (=chandelier)　吊灯
percentage of rejects　不合格率
permanent address　永久住址
personal effects　私人用品
personnel department　人事部
piecework wage　计件工资
PIM（personal information management）个人信息管理
place of issue　颁发地点
portfolio investment　间接投资，组合投资，证券投资
position applied for　申请的职位
position desired　期望的职位
post doctorate　博士后
postal service　邮局服务处
postpone/put off an appointment　推迟约会
precise writer　记录（员）
probation period　试用期，见习期
processing with imported materials　进料加工
processing with supplied materials　来料加工
processing with supplied sample　来样加工
product title　产品名称
production department　生产部
production line　生产线
promote business relationship　促进业务关系
promoted to　被提升为
proposed as　被提名为
prospects of promotion　晋升机会
protective gear　防护装备
public relations department　公关部
public servant　公务员
purchasing department　采购部
quality control department　质量管理部
quality controller　质量管理员
raw material　原料
reach an agreement　达成协议
reactivate business relationship　使业务关系重新活跃起来
reference letter　推荐信
refresher course　进修课程
register book　旅客登记簿
registered capital　注册资本
registration form　登记表
reliable quality　质量可靠
reliable reputation　信誉可靠
reschedule an appointment　重新安排约会
research and development department　研发部
restore/renew business relationship　恢复业务关系
return ticket　回程票
rocking chair　摇椅
room key　房间钥匙
room number　房间号码
round-trip ticket　往返机票
safe firm　可靠的公司
safety goggle　护目镜
sales by sample　凭样品买卖
sales department　销售部
sales rep (representative)　销售代表
sales strategy　销售战略
sample for reference　参考样品
sash window　上下拉动的窗户，框格窗
satisfaction of customers　顾客的满意程度
scope of cooperation　合作范围

screw-type bulb　螺口灯泡
sell like hotcakes　大卖
semi-conductor system　半导体生产系统
service exports and imports　服务进出口
shop assistant　售货员
shorthand typist　速记打字员
shower bath (=shower)　淋浴
showy goods　外观华丽的商品
simultaneous interpreter　同声译员
single bed　单人床
single room　单人房
skilled worker　技术工人
skillful manufacture　制作精巧
sliding scale　浮动计算（法），（工资、税收等）按比例增减
smoking set　烟具
smuggled goods　走私货
social activity　社会活动
social practice　社会实践
sofa/settee　长沙发
sophisticated technology　工艺精良
specialize in　专营
speed up business relationship　加快业务关系的发展
square meter　平方米
staff recruitment　雇员招聘，员工招聘
staffing level　人员编制
stamp duty　印花税
step out　暂时离开
superior quality　品质优异
system analyst　系统分析员
take on　雇佣，承担（工作），呈现（面貌）
tea table　茶几
technological cooperation　技术合作
telephone typist　打字员
temporary job　临时工作
through the courtesy of　经……的介绍
tie up　（工作等）把……缠住，使无法脱身
tip-top quality　第一流的质量
toilet roll/toilet paper　卫生纸，手纸
toner cartridge　调色块，碳粉匣
top-grade goods　头等货
towel rail/towel rack　毛巾架
trade reputation　贸易声誉
trade with　和……进行贸易
training department　培训部
transit duty　过境税
TV product placement　电视植入广告
unanimous approval　一致的赞同
unfinished products　半成品
visible trade　有形贸易
wage index　工资指数
wages and salaries department　薪酬部
wall lamp　壁灯
waste-paper basket　废纸篓
water closet (WC)　厕所，抽水马桶
weekly wage　周工资
wicker chair　藤椅
wide varieties　品种繁多
with a right to vote　有表决权
working hours　工作时间
working meeting　例会
X-ray machine　X光机与酒店

References
参 考 文 献

[1] 陈丹, 浩瀚. 商务英语多变表达[M]. 北京: 中国水利水电出版社, 2008.
[2] 东方友人. 商务美语[M]. 北京: 世界图书出版公司, 2002.
[3] 高悦伶. 商贸英语脱口说[M]. 北京: 中国宇航出版社, 2005.
[4] 浩瀚. 商务英语情景会话模板[M]. 北京: 国防工业出版社, 2007.
[5] 李硕. 流畅商务英语口语[M]. 大连: 大连理工大学出版社, 2009.
[6] 吕映霞. 外企实用英语口语[M]. 北京: 金盾出版社, 2006.
[7] 阮绩智. 国际商务英语听说[M]. 杭州: 浙江大学出版社, 2006.
[8] 孙亚捷, 刘东浩. 赴美国口语[M]. 天津: 天津大学出版社, 2002.
[9] 孙耀远. 商务英语听说教练[M]. 大连: 大连理工大学出版社, 2007.
[10] 王艳. 全方位商务英语口语[M]. 北京: 对外经济贸易大学出版社, 2005.
[11] 王玉章, 王怡. 商务英语会话[M]. 天津: 天津大学出版社, 2005.
[12] 张中倩. 求职英语一日通[M]. 北京: 科学出版社, 2005.
[13] 韩经伦. 管理学英语: 口语与听力训练[M]. 天津: 南开大学出版社, 2006.
[14] 李红. 每天一课英语口语短句365[M]. 大连: 大连理工大学出版社, 2008.
[15] 许勤超. 实用英语开口说[M]. 青岛: 中国海洋大学出版社, 2004.
[16] 李国庆, 袁泉. MP3全能版商务英语从入门到提高[M]. 北京: 中国宇航出版社, 2008.
[17] 邓长慧. 外企白领应用英语口语[M]. 北京: 中国国际广播出版社, 2008.